T0128747

Prophet Muhammad (S) And His Family

A Sociological Perspective

Revised Edition

by

Shamim Aleem

authorHOUSE®

AuthorHouse™
1663 Liberty Drive
Bloomington, IN 47403
www.authorhouse.com
Phone: 1-800-839-8640

First edition published in 2007
First published by AuthorHouse 10/20/2011
IInd Print: I.B.S. (India) March 2008
ISBN: 978-1-4670-2819-6 (sc)
ISBN: 978-1-4670-2818-9 (e)

DEDICATED
TO
THE YOUNG GENERATION

May this humble presentation promote a better understanding
among the youth of the essence of the life and message of
Prophet Muhammad (S). May they be inspired to follow
the traits and traditions of the Prophet and fill their lives
with love, kindness and a commitment to peace.

I have left amongst you the Book of Allah and the Sunnah of His messenger which if you hold fast, you shall never go astray.

Khutaba Hajjal-ul-Wada Farewell address.
9th Dhual-Hijjah 10 AH,(6th March 632 A. D.)

Table of Contents

A Note on Second Edition

In this second edition, I have made an attempt to place before the readers, a more authentic and detail information about the life of the Prophet Muhammad(S).

In the process of revision of this book, Mr.Farooq Ansari(Westborough, Massachusetts) introduced me to Dr.Mohammad Yousaf(Westborough, Massachusetts) I am thankful to him for this. Brother Mohammad Yusuf is a sincere, honest and dedicated person. He is well versed with the details of Islamic history. His love for Sirah is great. I have no words to appreciate his selfless service in bringing out this volume.My daughter Nazneen Khan helped me in incorporating the changes. May God reward her for this work.

I look forward to the readers for a feedback.

August 2011   Shamim Aleem
                                    Email: shamimaleem@hotmail.com

Preface

Over the past 1400-years, literally thousands of books have been written, both by believers and non-believers on the different aspects of the life of the Prophet Muhammad (S). Even then it cannot be claimed that a true and exhaustive picture of his multidimensional life has been successfully projected. The gaps in the narratives call for the attention of serious minded researchers.

It is no doubt a great honor, to include one's name in the list of the biographers of the Prophet. It is also a great responsibility to present an accurate picture of his personality. Writers have often become so emotionally charged in their praise as to lose sight of objectivity. Some have turned critical of his life style. Non-believers, in particular were critical of his private life, especially of the part spent in Madina. After the establishment of an Islamic State, there was not much ground for criticism of his policies. Some writers however accused him of having resorted to forceful conversion and permitting the practice of slavery.

Many focused attention on his family life and found his multiple marriages the butt of denigration. They could not understand the reasons behind these marriages, and took a negative view of them.

In the last few years and especially after 9/11, interest in Islam and Islamic literature has increased tremendously. Non-believers are in a dilemma. On one hand, Islam is supposed to be a religion of peace, while on the other; terrorism associated with Muslims is on the rise. By making an attempt to depict an objective picture of the life of Prophet Muhammad(S), I have tried to underline the fact that Islam is not a religion of violence but of peace, and the life of the Prophet provides convincing evidence of this.

I am neither a student of history nor of Islamic studies. I belong to the discipline of Social Science. I have tried to look at his family life from a sociological perspective, an approach different from that of other writers. Since Sunnah, the traditions of the Prophet have been meticulously recorded by his followers; it holds a special significance in the life of Muslims. They are expected to acquire good knowledge of the private life of the Prophet. For the purpose of composing this book I had to undertake a deeper study of Sunnah. I could not read the original Arabic literature, as my knowledge of that language is limited. I thus had to rely on Urdu and English translations. When I started making a study of the subject, I found that there are numerous gaps and contradictions in regard to the private life of the Prophet. For instance, Prophet's date of birth was correctly recorded though he was like any other child of Quraish tribe. Not only that, the dates of the marriages of his father, Abdullah and his grandfather, Abdul Muttalib, have also been recorded, but after three decades, when it came to the Prophet's own children, there is a lot of confusion. There is no authentic record about the number of his sons, the sequence of his children, and the age at which they died, to mention only a few.

Historians are quite sure about the dates of the deaths of his mother Amina and grandfather Abdul Muttalib, but confusion prevails over the deaths of his beloved wife Khadijah and his dear uncle Abu Talib. Further, there is no unanimity about the gap between the First and the Second Revelations of Quran. It has been put between a few weeks to two and a half years. Similarly different authors have given different time periods about his stay at Quba on his way to Madina. Most surprising is the fact that *Ila*, the temporary separation of the Prophet with his wives for one month, which was a significant event in his life, has not been recorded accurately. Some believe it was in 5th AH while some others claim that this event took place in 9th AH. All this confusion is in spite of the fact that his companions and his wife Aisha, who has many traditions to her credit, were with him all the time. Of late, Aisha's age has become another controversial topic.

When I look at all these things, I feel somewhat disheartened. For Islam is the second largest religion of the world, with a population of about 1.3 billion. There are more than 56 countries where Muslims are in majority. Economically, several of these countries are fairly rich. In spite of these favorable factors, Muslims are far behind in the field of research. Books by Muslim writers keep appearing on various aspects of Islam but not many reflect the required level of scholarship. In order to overcome these controversies, what is needed is to go deep into the original sources to have a correct picture of of the private life of the Prophet. As I have my own limitations I look forward to future researchers to give a serious thought on these issues.

My attempt to depict the life of the Prophet is a very modest one. My aim is to place at the disposal of young English speaking people, a wider view of the family life of the Prophet, so that they learn something from it to make their own lives more fruitful and happy. If I succeed in this, it would be a cause of joy in my life. The book may be of source of interest to those non-Muslims too who are keen to know more about Islam. I hope it will also be a valuable contribution to women studies.

In my efforts to write this book, I have received encouragement and help from various quarters. Although it is difficult to thank them all by name I must mention at least a few names. When the idea to write on this topic came to my mind, the first person with whom I discussed was Mufti Sayeed of Pakistan who was on a visit to the USA. His encouragement helped me in undertaking the project. Abidullah Ghazi of IQRA was also a source of encouragement to me. Prof. Mohsin Usmani, of Central Institute of English and Foreign Languages, Hyderabad, a renowned scholar and a man of extensive writings on Islamic literature has generously spared his valuable time in going through the first and the final drafts of my book. I am highly indebted to him. I am also grateful to Arif Hussaini (California) a civil servant of international repute and an author of many books who has taken great pains in going through the final draft of the book.

For the collection of information, I had to look into many public and private libraries. Hafiz Rabbani Ahmed of IAGD, Michigan and Mahmood Akbar from Michigan have very good personal collections and both of them kept their libraries at my disposal.

I must acknowledge the help and support of my friends and well wishers like Padma Shree Mujtaba Hussain, a well known Urdu writer and columnist of international repute, Hasan Chishti (Chicago), poet and a person of extraordinary generosity, Prof. Shahid Ali Abbasi, Head of the Dept. of Islamic Studies, Osmania University, Hyderabad and my young nephew, Rehan Khan (Canada.)

The typing of the manuscript had taken place in Hyderabad, which was definitely a very strenuous job. It would not have been possible without the help of my dear old student Dr. Kaneez Zehra, lecturer in Public Administration, Maulana Azad National Urdu University, Hyderabad and her hard working husband Zubain Hussain.

It was my family support that gave me encouragement to complete the work. My son Saleem Mohammad and my daughter- in- law Sofia, my daughters, Yasmeen and Nazneen and their husbands, Dr. Mahmood Ali Khan and Asad Raza Khan were always a source of constant support to me. My eldest grandson, Nabeel, a 12-year old student of HUDA Islamic School, was always keen to contribute his share of knowledge. I appreciate his spirit. I only pray to God that my book may be a source of inspiration to all of them and to make their lives more purposeful.

May 2007

Shamim Aleem
Email: shamimaleem@hotmail.com

Part I

From Birth To Prophethood

Islam is the second largest religion in the world today. Although it has a history of only fourteen hundred years, during this short period it has spread to every nook and corner of the world. The Muslim population in the world today is about 1.3 billion. Muslims are in majority in 56 countries. One in every five persons in the world believes in Islam.

In the pre-Islamic era, the whole world had been in darkness. The political and socio-economic conditions in most parts of the world were extremely bad. There was tyranny and terrorism. There were continuous wars. Might was right. The common man was badly suppressed and the concept of equality was missing. A person could not even raise his voice against any injustice done to him. The social fabric was extremely weak and there were no established social norms based on morality. In this era of darkness, the holy books had earlier predicted the arrival of a new prophet, who would show the right path to humanity. However, nobody even imagined that he would come from one of the most backward regions of the world, Arabia. Arabia was mostly a desert and a network of barren mountains. The Arabs were divided into a number of tribes. At the advent of Islam, the two main inhabitants of Arabia were Banu Qahata and Banu Ishme. In addition to these tribes, there were Jews. The population was both nomadic and sedentary. The tribes were divided into small groups, each headed by a powerful chief. The bonds within the group were so strong that the tribesmen would go out of their way to support their men, even when they were wrong. The weak used to take shelter under the strong.

It was in this background that the Prophet Muhammad(S) was entrusted with the responsibility of lifting humanity from a state of darkness to a state of enlightenment. His mission was not confined to any particular region, but to the world as a whole, as it is mentioned in the Quran.

Say O mankind, I am the Rasool of Allah towards all of you.
Al-Araf: 7:158

O! Muhammad, we have not sent you but
as a blessing for all the Worlds.
Al-Anbiya: 21: 107

Prophet Muhammad(S) belonged to the Quraish tribe, the ancestry of which goes back to Prophet Ismail, son of Prophet Ibrahim. The custody of the Kabah, the shrine in Mecca was traditionally vested in the Chief of Quraish and passed on through hereditary succession. The Prophet's grandfather, Abdul Muttalib was from the renowned Hashim clan within the Quraish tribe. He was respected by all for his generosity, trustworthiness and wisdom. He was the custodian of the Kabah and was responsible for re-discovering the Zamzam spring, which had lost its track when the Jhurum were forced to vacate Mecca. When Abdul Muttalib got the indication to dig a well, the people did not come forward to help him, and he had only one son to help him. He felt miserable and prayed to God that if he had ten sons, he would sacrifice one of them to Al Kabah.[1] God fulfilled his desire and gave him ten sons. The youngest son was Abdullah, father of Prophet Muhammad(S). When Abdul Muttalib's sons reached adulthood, he went to fulfill his vow to sacrifice one of his sons. Lots were drawn and the name of Abdullah came, but his life was saved by sacrificing one hundred camels.

The popularity of the Kabah had created jealousy and resentment among many who did not accept Kabah as the place of worship. An Abyssinian, Viceroy of Yemen, Abrahah, built a magnificent cathedral at Sana to divert pilgrims from Mecca to Sana. Knowing his intention, some of the tribes became furious. One man went inside the church and desecrated it. This made Abrahah lose his temper and he vowed to destroy the Kabah. So he invaded Mecca with an army of 6000 warriors, including many elephants.[2] The biggest elephant, on which Abrahah was riding, knelt down at a place near Kabah and refused to move forward. In the meantime, God sent His aid, in the form of birds carrying three stones each, and dropping on the army.The stones were so sharp that they injured the soldiers and killed many of them. Thus, he could not succeed in his attempt to destroy Kabah as God saved His House. This year (571 AD) was known as the Year of the Elephant.

When Abdullah was twenty-five years old, Abdul Muttalib decided to get him married. He was very handsome and was called Yusuf (Joseph) of his time. Abdul Muttalib chose Amina, the daughter of Wahb, as the bride. As her father had died, her uncle, Wahaby became her guardian. It is interesting to know that Wahaby also had a daughter by the name Halah. Abdul Muttalib chose her for himself.[3] Both marriages took place on the same day in 569 AD.

Immediately after his marriage, Abdullah went on a trade visit to Palestine and Syria. On his way back, he fell sick and died in Yathrib (Madina). It is generally agreed that his death occurred two months before the birth of the Prophet. Abdullah had left five camels herd of sheep, and a slave girl Barakha, who was later on known as Umm Ayman, to take care of the Prophet.

The only consolation for Amina was the unborn child of Abdullah. A few days before the delivery, she heard a voice telling her that "Thou carriest in thy womb the lord of this people, and when he is born say I place him beneath the protection of the One from the evil of every envier, then name him Muhammad".[4] Muhammad was born in the lunar month of Rabi-ul-Awal, in the Year of the Elephant (571 AD). However, there is a difference of opinion on the exact date. It is generally believed to be 12th, but according to scholar Md. Sulaiman Al Mansourpuri, and the astrologer Muhmud Pasha, it was 9th Rabi-ul-Awal.[5] He was named Muhammad even though it was an uncommon name. Abdul Muttalib was very happy on the birth of the child and immediately took him to Kabah and prayed to God. Thuwaiba, the slave girl of his uncle Abu Lahab nursed him for the first few days after which he was entrusted to Halima, a wet-nurse. The Arabs living in town had the custom of sending their new born to the desert to be taken care by the Bedouin tribe. It was not just to provide fresh air and to prevent infant mortality but it was also for their spiritual upliftment as well as for acquiring pure characteristics and language. Some of the tribes like Bani Sad bin Bakr for instance had a high reputation for rearing children. Halima bint Abu Dhuaib, from Bani Sad bin Bakr tribe, was entrusted with the responsibility of nursing Muhammad. Her husband Al-Harith bin Abdul Azza was also from the same tribe.

In the beginning, Halima was not willing to take care of Muhammad, as he was an orphan. For the Bedouin, the motive of rearing children was not short-term monetary gain but was for the purpose of establishing a lifetime relationship between the child and foster mother. The foster mother could then look to this child for favor and support in her later life. As Halima could not get any other child, she decided to take Muhammad.

The moment Halima accepted him her luck seemed to change for the better. Halima is reported to have said, "It was a year of drought and famine, and we had nothing to eat. I rode on a brown she-ass. We also had with us an old she-camel. By Allah, we could not get even a drop of milk. There was not enough milk in my breast and even the she camel had nothing to feed my son. When I put Muhammad on my breast, to my great surprise, I found enough milk in it. My husband then went to the she camel to milk it and to his astonishment; he found plenty of milk." [6] The presence of Muhammad continued to shower blessings on her family. Halima was so happy with the presence of Muhammad that she did not want to part with him and pleaded for permission to keep him for another two years to which Amina agreed.

When Muhammad was about four years old, an unusual incident took place that scared Halima so much that she took the boy back to his mother. Muhammad himself described the event in the following words "There came unto me two men clothed in white, with a golden basin full of snow, then they laid hold on me and splitting open my breast they brought forth my heart. This likewise they split open and took from it a black clot, which they cast away. Then they washed my heart and my breast with snow".[7*]

Many historians do not believe this story. They believe that the life of the Prophet is free of any irrational or mysterious.

Muhammad returned to his mother. When he was six years old, his mother decided to take him to Yathrib (Madina) to meet her relatives. On the way back, she fell sick and died in Abwa, a place between Madina and Mecca. Her slave girl Barakah, brought Muhammad back to Madina.[8]

After his mother's death, he came under the guardianship of his grandfather Abdul Muttalib, who loved him immensely. Abdul Muttalib used to go to Kabah everyday and sit for long hours. He always used to take Muhammad along with him.He used to sit on a cushion laid down in the shade of the Kabah.His children would sit around that cushion, but Abdul Muttalib would bring Muhammad close to him, to sit on the cushion.

Originally, the Arab community believed in the Oneness of God. The Kabah was a center of attraction not only for Meccans, but people from all parts of Arabia who flocked to it for pilgrimage. However, with the passage of time the theory of Oneness of God was corrupted. Idols were brought who acted as mediators between men and God. There were 360 idols inside Kabah, some of them like Hubel, Manat, Nasr, and Uzza were considered very strong. Neither Abdul Muttalib nor Muhammad ever prayed to these idols.

Abdul Muttalib died when Muhammad was eight years old. He then came under the guardianship of his uncle Abu Talib, who was his father's real brother. Abu Talib was a person of limited means. Moreover, he had many children and he could not give him the comforts of life, but he gave him his love and affection in abundance. Although Abu Talib did not adopt the faith of his nephew, he gave his support and protection to Muhammad till the end.

Right from his childhood, Muhammad was unlike other boys. He never indulged in activities that boys of his age would participate in. He narrated how once or twice he went to the city to have fun like other boys, but God did not want him to indulge in such activities and he consequently fell asleep.

When Muhammad was about twelve years old, he went on a business trip to Syria along with his uncle Abu Talib. When they reached Busra, they met a monk by the name of Bahira. He recognized Muhammad and said, "This is the master of all humans. Allah will send him with a Message, which will be a mercy to all beings." He also asked Abu Talib to send the boy back to Mecca for fear of the Jews.[9]

Muhammad did not have any formal education. He could not read or write, but he had an abundance of knowledge. He had some training in the use of weapons of war along with his uncles Abbas and Hamza. Hamza was a man of mighty stature, great strength and was a very good swordsman. Muhammad was of average strength, but had an aptitude for archery. In those days, there were no big wars. The Quraish were involved in only a few small ones and hence the youth did not have any experience of wars.

Muhammad did not have any specific job, but it was reported that he worked for some time as a shepherd for Bani Sad in Mecca.[10] Abu Talib used to take him on business trips that gave him a lot of experience. Soon he was known for his honesty, integrity and experience. When he was about twenty years old, he developed affection for his cousin Fakhitah (later on known as Umm Hani) and wanted to marry her, but Abu Talib had different plans for her so he politely refused.[11]

When Muhammad was about twenty-five years old, a wealthy widow of Mecca, Khadijah, who was in her forties, employed him as her agent to trade on her behalf. He went to Syria along with her servant Maysarah. He made double the normal profit for her. Maysarah was greatly impressed by his honesty, sincerity and behavior. He narrated every thing to Khadijah. Khadijah, who had refused many matrimonial offers by well-known persons of Mecca, developed a liking for him and desired to make him her life partner. Muhammad agreed to her proposal and they were married. Muhammad moved to her house, as he did not have a house of his own. They lived a happy married life for twenty-five years. They had six children, two boys and four girls. The girls survived, but the boys died in their infancy.

Muhammad had great respect in society. He was known as Al Ameen (trustworthy) and Al Sadiq (truthful). People had respect for him because of his noble character and his behavior. When Muhammad was thirty-five years old, the Quraish decided to re-build the Kabah. A controversy arose on who would pick up the heavenly black stone to put it back in its place in the shrine. It was suggested by the oldest among the tribal chiefs that the one who entered the Kabah first, should be made the arbitrator. All accepted this proposal and all eyes were at the door. When Muhammad entered the Kabah, every one accepted him as arbitrator. Muhammad asked for a cloth, which he spread on the ground and placed the stone in its center. Then he asked the representatives of different clans to lift the cloth supporting the stone together. Then he laid the stone in its proper position with his own hands. The wise decision of Muhammad solved the problem in a peaceful way, which otherwise could have turned into a serious conflict.[12]

To conclude, the life of Muhammad before Prophethood was generally smooth. Although he was an orphan, he had an abundance of love from his extended family. After his marriage with Khadijah, he led a happy family life.

The Prophethood

Culturally different parts of Arabia differed greatly from one another. There were some places such as Yemen that had once reached the zenith of civilization. However, in general, historians referred to the pre-Islamic era of Arabia as a period of Jahiliyyah (ignorance) or the age of darkness. Not that they were bad people. They had many good qualities, but on the whole the social and moral values had degenerated to the lowest ebb possible. For example, there was no restriction on sexual relations. There was no limit on the number of wives a men could have. A man could marry two sisters at the same time or even the wives of his father if divorced or widowed.[13]Some of the customs were barbaric in nature, such as the burying of newborn girls. Even though the Kabah was the house of Allah, inside it were idols. Idol worship was the order of the day. The level of literacy was extremely low. Music and poetry had a very high place in society.

Right from his childhood, Muhammad had no interest in local customs of ignorance. He was deeply distressed with the existing state of affairs. Gradually, he started preferring solitude. Much before the First Revelation of Quran, it was his routine to go to a cave called Hira, two miles away from Mecca for meditation. He used to spend days alone in the cave, taking some food with him for sustenance. Sometimes, Khadijah also used to get some food for him. She never objected to his staying there.

The First Revelation

The First Revelation was not all of a sudden. He was slowly getting mentally prepared for it. Once, in the last days of Ramadan, though there is no agreement on the exact date, he was sleeping in the cave of Hira when the First Revelation came to him. The Prophet himself had narrated this. He said, "As I was sleeping the angel Gabriel came to me and said, "Read".

"I do not read, I replied. He forcefully squeezed me, till I thought I would die. Then he released me and said, "Read". Again I said I do not read He again took and squeezed me until I thought I would die. Again he said, "Read." I said, what shall I read? Then he said,

Read in the name of your Lord who created - created man from a clot. Read your Lord is the most Gracious. Who taught by the pen, taught man what he knew not.
Al-Alaq: 96:1-5

Muhammad was badly shaken. He did not know whether to believe it or not. It was like a dream to him. He immediately proceeded to his home. As he was going home, he again saw Gabriel in the sky, saying, "You are the Messenger of God and I am Gabriel." With great difficulty he came home. He was shivering terribly. He asked his wife to cover him with blankets. Khadijah was a very mature lady. She knew him intimately. She understood his feelings. She believed his statement. She immediately took him to her cousin Waraqah bin Nawfal, who was a Christian scholar of scriptures and was old and blind. On the basis of his knowledge, he confirmed what Gabriel had said. He also predicted that Muhammad would be tortured by his people and would be forced to leave his city.

After the First Revelation, there were no more Revelations for some time. It is reported that many a time the Prophet used to get frustrated and felt like throwing himself from the mountain. There is a difference of opinion about the time gap between the First and the Second Revelations. Some authentic sources believe that it was a gap of only a few weeks, while others say that there was a hiatus of two years or more. [14]There was also a difference of opinion as to which Surah was second in chronological order. According to many traditions, it was Al-Muddaththir.[15]

O Muddaththir! (the one enveloped - one of the titles of the Prophet Muhammad) Stand up and warn. Proclaim the greatness of your Lord, purify your clothes, keep yourself away from uncleanliness do not favor others to expect again and be patient for the sake of your Lord.
Al-Muddaththir: 74:1-7

In the First Revelation, the Prophet was not told of the great mission that was being entrusted to him. But in the Second Revelation, when he was mentally prepared, he was given the idea of his great mission. He was commanded to rise and warn the people about the consequences of the way of life they were leading and to proclaim the greatness of Allah in a place where others were being idolized. This mission required that his life be dedicated to carrying out the duty of reforming his people. In the end, he was asked to be patient in view of the hardship and trouble that he might have to face while performing his duties.

During the course of Revelation, many a time there was anxiety and distress in the Prophet's mind. Some times he had doubts that God had forsaken him and that He was displeased with him. To give reassurance to him, God revealed the Surah of Ad-Dhuha.

> ***By the morning daylight and by the night, when it covers with darkness, your Lord has neither forsaken you, O Muhammad, nor is He displeased. Certainly the latter period shall be better for you than the earlier.***
> ***Ad-Dhuha: 93:1-4***

The Prophet then continued his mission with greater enthusiasm. Although Revelations were kept a secret from the public, he started sharing them with his near and dear ones. One day, Gabriel came and taught him how to perform ablution and prayer. The Prophet came home and prayed with his wife Khadijah. Islam was now established. Khadijah had the honor to be the first Muslim, after the Prophet. Ali, ten-year-old cousin of the Prophet, Zayd his adopted son and Abu Bakr his close friend followed her. Abu Bakr was an influential man. He enjoyed great respect in society. He tried to spread the message within his close circle. However, this process was very slow and he could convert only a few.

Then the Quranic revelation came,

> ***Admonish your close relatives.***
> ***Ash-Shuara: 26:214***

The Prophet invited his relatives for dinner, but before he could say anything they dispersed. The next day, he again invited them and spoke about his new faith. Although the response was not very encouraging, it was not negative, except from his uncle, Abu Lahab, who openly opposed him. For three years, the Prophet worked on his mission in secret. However,

Meccans came to know about it and were worried. Then the Revelation came to make it public.

Proclaim publicly what you are commanded
and turn away from mushrikeen.
Al-Hijr: 15:94

After this Revelation, the Prophet started addressing the people publicly concerning idolatry and preaching Oneness of God. When he started preaching the new religion, many people started doubting his honesty, sincerity and the state of his mind. God at many places in the Quran had made it clear that the Quran was neither his innovation nor he a mad person.

By the star when it sets, your companion (Muhammad)
is neither astray, nor misguided, nor does he speak out of
his own desire. This is but an inspired revelation.
An Najam: 53: 1-4

By the grace of your Lord, you are not a madman
and you shall have a never-ending reward
.Al-Qulam: 68: 2, 3

--- Surely this word (the Quran) is brought by a noble
Messenger (Gabriel) possessor of mighty power, having
very high rank with the owner of the Throne (Allah) --- O
people of Makkah, your companion has not gone mad --
The Quran is not the word of an accursed Shaitan.
Al Takwir: 81: 19-25

The Quraish did not approve of the new faith. The main reasons for their opposition was that Islam was attempting to annihilate their gods, who for hundreds of years were believed to have answered their popular prayers, and accepting Islam meant their forefathers were wrong, and above all, it challenged their political and financial power. These gods witnessed foreheads rubbed every day at their feet in reverent worship.

The Quran spoke of them

> *Surely, you (O Mushrikeen) and your deities that you worship besides Allah shall be the fuel of hell; therein you shall all enter.*
> *Al-Anbiya: 21:98*

Many of the Quraish were honest men. They were opposed to Islam on the matter of principles that they believed in. They wanted to settle the matter peacefully, so they approached Abu Talib and complained to him about the Prophet. Abu Talib sent them away with pacifying words, but their cause of grievance persisted. The Prophet would not desist from doing his duty. Another delegation of Quraish dignitaries approached Abu Talib, complaining that his nephew was insulting their gods and labeling their ancestors as misguided fools. The Prophet continued preaching as usual. The Quraish could not think of murdering him but they continued teasing him in every possible way. When they could not stop him, they tried to compromise. They offered that if he worshiped their gods for a year, they would worship his God for a year. It was at that time that Surah Al-Kafirun was revealed.

> *Say: O unbelievers! I worship not that whom you worship, nor will you worship that whom I worship. I shall never worship those deities, whom you worship, nor will you ever worship Allah, whom I worship, to you be your religion and to me mine.*
> *Al-Kafirun: 109: 1-6*

The Quraish formed an association headed by the Prophet's uncle Abu Lahab, to adopt the meanest methods possible to harass him. Abu Lahab himself tried to obstruct the way of the Prophet. He also inflicted physical torture. His wife Umm Jamil joined him in his efforts. Then the Quranic Revelation naming Abu Lahab, the enemy of Islam came. It may be noted that he was the only person who has been condemned by name in the Quran.

> *Perish the hands of Abu Lahab! And perish he! His wealth and whatever he earned did not avail him anything. Soon he shall be burnt in a flaming fire and his wife the carrier of crackling fire wood shall have a rope of palm leaf fibre around her neck.*
> *Al-Lahab: 111:1-5*

Abu Lahab continued his opposition, choosing to disregard this divine

11

admonishment. The believers were treated in an inhuman manner and it was becoming very difficult for them to live there. In the mean time, God revealed Surah Al-Kahaf and the Surah Az Zumar, giving indication of migration.

When the Prophet came to know about Ashamah Negus, king of Abyssinia, a fair ruler, he gave permission to his followers to take asylum there. In the fifth year of Prophethood, in the month of Rajab, a group of twelve men and four women left for Abyssinia. Among the immigrants were Uthman bin Affan and Ruqayya (the Prophet's son-in-law and daughter), Umm Salamah (who was later on married to the Prophet, after the death of her first husband) along with her husband Abu Salamah. The Quraish were perturbed at this step and although they tried their best to persuade the king of Abyssinia to expel the immigrants, they did not succeed. Frustrated, the Quraish decided to kill the Prophet. They went to Abu Talib with the proposal that they would give him a young boy to be adopted as his son in lieu of his nephew Muhammad, whom they wanted to kill. Abu Talib became furious and told them to do whatever they wanted but he would protect his nephew.[16]

The Quraish tried different ways of killing the Prophet. One morning in the sixth year of Prophethood, when the Prophet prostrated for prayers, Abu Jahal took a big rock with the intention of killing the Prophet with it. He was scared away by a ferocious camel before he could accomplish his nefarious task. Thus God saved the Prophet. It was in the same year that two strong stalwarts, Hamza the Prophet's uncle, and Umar bin Khattab embraced Islam. These two men strengthened Prophet's hands. Apart from their conversion, a few important incidents took place within a few weeks. The Quraish sent their representatives to negotiate with the Prophet. Utbah bin Rabia, a chief among them, approached the Prophet and offered to give him anything, wealth, kingship, and the most beautiful girl to marry, provided he stopped proclaiming his new faith. In reply to their demand, the Prophet started reciting Surahs from the Quran. His reply was obvious.

Sh'ib Abu Talib

Abu Talib, anticipating a serious situation, called the kinsfolk of bani Hashim and bani Al-Muttalib to protect and defend Muhammad. Although many of them including Abu Talib had not accepted his religion, all of them responded positively. Abu Lahab was the only person who sided with the disbelieving Quraish against his own clan, which was against Arab traditions. The Quraish were badly frustrated. They knew that if Muhammad was killed, there would be bloodshed. They decided on a social boycott. Business dealings, intermarriage, even verbal contact would discontinue until the Prophet was given to them to be killed.

Abu Talib sensed the gravity of the situation and withdrew to a valley on the outskirts of Mecca, with the result that the families of Bani Hashim and Bani Muttalib were confined within a narrow mountain pass (Sh'ib of Abu Talib) that was the hereditary property of Bani Hashim. They were confined there from the beginning of Muharram in the seventh year of Prophethood till the tenth year. This period of three years was a period of great hardship as even the supply of food was stopped. Many times they had to survive on leaves of trees and skins of animals. The cries of hungry children could be heard from a distance, but the idolaters were not moved by their sufferings. The Prophet did not lose heart and continued to go to the Kabah and perform prayers. After three years of blockade, the pact was broken with the help of God – ants had eaten away almost the entire document, except the name of God.

The Year of Sorrow

Due to these three years of physical and mental strain, Abu Talib had become very weak and fell sick. He passed away a few months later. It was a great shock to the Prophet, as he had been his supporter for forty years and loved him more than his own children. It was because of him that the Quraish were scared to take any drastic step against the Prophet. Only a few months after the death of his uncle, the Prophet had another great loss. He lost his beloved wife Khadijah.[17] He Prophet lost both the pillars on which he had relied so far.

Suffering Of The Prophet After The Death Of Abu Talib

With the death of Abu Talib, the Quraish had a free hand, as they knew that there is no one to protect Muhammad. They accelerated their sinister pursuits against him. They tried various means to humiliate him and even physically torture him. Mambit-al-Azdi narrated that one day when the Prophet was reciting *La illaha illal lah* in the Kabah, some people threw dust on his face while others continuously abused and molested him.[18] Ibn-al-As narrated that once the Prophet was performing *salat* in

Kabah, Aqabah ibn Abi Muait came and pulling a sheet of cloth around the Prophet's neck, started to strangulate him. Abu Bakr, a close companion of the Prophet, happened to be there, he pulled Aqaba away. Abdullah ibn Masud narrated that once when the Messenger of Allah was performing *salat* in the Mosque, Abu Jahal instigated some persons to throw the entrails of a camel over him. Aqabah ibn Ali Muhit, the most wretched man among them, put the entrails over the shoulders of the Prophet when he was in *Sajadah*.[19]

The Prophet's Visit to Al-Taif

As the Prophet was not hopeful of bringing a change in the life of Meccan, he moved to Taif, a place sixty kilometers from Mecca, hoping that the people of Taif would protect him and help him. However, contrary to his hopes, they treated him most contemptuously. In the Prophet's own words, as narrated by Aisha, "the hardest day for me was the day of Al Aqabah" (the day when he visited Taif). [20]

It was Shawwal (May/June 619 AD) when he left for Taif, accompanied by Zayd bin Haritha. He stayed there for ten days, making great efforts to convey his message to the people. However, not only did the people not listen to him, they also put him to severe mental and physical torture. Urea bin Zubain narrated that the people sat down on the road in two rows with stones in their hands. They pelted stones at him resulting in injury. Blood was flowing profusely from his feet, [21] and with great difficulty, he left the city. As Abu Talib was not there, he had to request somebody else for protection to enter the city of Mecca. Al Mutim Adi, a notable of Mecca, offered protection to the Prophet. He asked his people to be fully armed and then asked Muhammad to enter the city[22]. This was the state of affairs of law and order at that time. A person who had been living in the city for the past fifty years, respected by society, known for his exemplary character could not enter his own hometown.

Depressed and heart broken, he prayed to God. When he was on his way back to Mecca, Allah sent Gabriel, together with the angel of the mountains who asked the permission of the Prophet to bury Mecca between Al Akhshabain – Abu Qubais and Qu'ayqa'an mountains. The Prophet replied that he would rather have some one from their loins who will worship Allah; the Almighty with no associate.[23] According to another tradition, Gabriel said that If Muhammed wanted he would blow the mountain over the people of Taif.

The Isra And Miraj — The Night Journey

One of the significant events in the life of the Prophet was his night journey from Mecca to Jerusalem and then to the heavens. Though there is no agreement on the exact date, it is generally believed that it was between twelve to sixteen months prior to migration to Madina. There is also no agreement whether it was a physical or spiritual experience. There is also a difference of opinion whether the Prophet saw Allah with his eyes or not. However, it is confirmed by different Surahs of Quran, like Surah Isra and Surah An-Najam that he did visit the heavens.

> *Glory to Him who took His devotee (Muhammad)*
> *one night from Al-Masjid-al-Haram (in Mecca) to Al-*
> *Masjid-al-Aqsa (in Jerusalem) whose vicinity We have*
> *blessed, so that We may show him some of our signs.*
> *Al-Isra: 17: 1*

> *His (Muhammad) own heart did not deny that which he*
> *saw. How can you O unbelievers then question what he*
> *saw? And he (Muhammad) saw him once again near Sidra-*
> *tul-Muntaha (the Lote tree at the end of the seven heavens,*
> *beyond which none can pass). Near it is Jann-tul-M'awa.*
> *An-Najm: 53: 11-15*

It was on this occasion that five prayers a day was made obligatory.

Hijra (Migration) to Madina

As Meccans could not be convinced of the new faith the Prophet decided to take his mission beyond the boundaries of Mecca. Every year during the period of Haj, people from different places used to come to Mecca. The Prophet taking advantage of this used to spread his message although there was always resistance from the Quraish.

In the tenth year of Propethood, six persons from Yathrib (Madina) embraced Islam. The main reason for their acceptance was that the Jews told them a Prophet would be coming soon. When these people went back, they started teaching Islam in their own city. This was the first step for taking the new faith beyond the boundaries of Mecca.

The following year, again on the occasion of the pilgrimage, another group of twelve persons accepted Muhammad as their Prophet. They took a pledge that was known as the First Aqabah Pledge. After this, the Prophet sent Musa'b bin Umair to Yathrib to give practical training in Islam. This had a great positive effect on the people of Yathrib, with the result that in the next pilgrimage, a large number of people, about seventy in total, made a Second Aqabah Pledge. These people were completely devoted to Islam and the Prophet. This gave rise to the establishment of an Islamic state.

Migration To Madina
Raby al awal 1 A.H. (September 622 AD.)

The conditions in Mecca deteriorated to such an extent that it was impossible for Muslims to live there any more. Considering the antagonism of the people of Mecca and the possibility of peaceful life in Madina, the Prophet gave permission to Muslims to migrate to Madina. Although this decision was made in secret, the Quraish came to know about it and were very much concerned.

Although Muslims had started migrating to Madina, the Prophet himself did not leave the city as he was waiting for orders from God. Then ultimately one night Gabriel came with the good news that the Prophet could migrate now. Gabriel also warned him of the anticipated danger to his life, and advised him not to sleep in his own bed. (Tabari Ibn Hasham). The Prophet asked Ali to sleep in his bed. That entire night the house of the Prophet was watched by his enemies who wanted to kill him, but with the help of God he could get out of the house without the knowledge of his enemies. Abu Bakr had made all the arrangements for migration. He also brought two camels for both of them but they did not go directly to Madina, as they knew that an intensive search would be made. They went to the cave of Thaur. Abu Bakr entered and checked all holes, lest any of them had a poisonous reptile. The Quraish had declared an award of 100 she-camels to anyone who would stop them. The Quraish came to the mouth of the cave also, but God protected them. After three days, they proceeded towards Madina.

The Propohet arrived at Quba on his way to Madina on 8th Rabi-ul-Awal 14 A.H, (*September 23rd 622 AD*) He stayed there for four days[25] and laid the foundation of the first Mosque to be built by Muslims. He offered the first Friday prayers and then left for Madina.

Welcome In Madina

The news of the Prophet's migration had spread far and wide. The people of Madina were in a jubilant mood and were anxiously waiting to welcome the Prophet. The streets were flooded with people waiting in the hot sun to have a glimpse of their beloved Prophet. Everyone was keen to be his host. But the Prophet waited for Allah's command. His she camel knelt down at the place where the great Mosque of Madina stands now. Abu Ayyub Ali Ansari had the good fortune of being his host, until the Prophet's own house was built.

The construction of the Mosque started at the very place where his camel had knelt down. The land belonged to two orphan boys. After paying for the land, construction of the Mosque started. Attached to the Mosque, the Prophet got two apartments constructed for his household, one for his second wife Sawda and another for Aisha, who was to join him soon.

In Madina, a new chapter of life began. In Mecca there was an atmosphere of fear, suspicion and hatred. Muslims were not able to come out openly and perform prayers in public. Life in Madina was different. It was a cosmopolitan city with different faiths, cultures and communities. It was more complex than in Mecca, especially due to the presence of several religions. Hence the Prophet had to face many problems. To mould the society of Madina into one united force was a very challenging job for the Prophet. The Prophet knew that this could not be achieved by force; it needed a strong and convincing religious faith.

The Prophet In The Battlefield

In Madina, the Prophet was acknowledged as both a religious and a political leader. He laid the foundation of an Islamic State but there were many hindrances in the way. There were three important Jewish tribes – Banu Qainuqua, Banu An-Nadir and Banu Qurazah. They were to be taken into confidence for the safeguard of their interests as well as the interests of the new Islamic State. This was not the end but the beginning of trouble. On the one hand, the Quraish were worried about the growing power and popularity of the new faith. They were desperately preparing plans to destroy the new state. Until this time, the Prophet had not waged war against any of his enemies, but he received Revelation to take arms against the unbelievers through Surah Al-Hajj.

Permission to fight back is hereby granted to the believers
against whom war is waged and because they are oppressed
certainly Allah has power to grant them victory.
Al-Hajj: 22:39

Although permission for war was given, it was neither desirable nor practical at that time to plunge into it directly. First, it was necessary to bring the commercial routes leading to Mecca under their control as these routes were always plundered by Quraish making the lives of Muslims miserable. It was also necessary to capture Meccan trade caravans in order to weaken the Meccan rulers financially.

Battle Of Badr
Ramadan, 2 AH (March 624 AD)

When the Prophet received the news that Abu Sufyan, a staunch opponent of Islam, was passing by Madina with his caravan carrying a lot of valuables, the Prophet himself led a campaign to intercept the caravan. Abu Sufyan was alert and got this news. He immediately sent a message to the Quraish in Mecca for help. The Quraish mustered an army of 1000 soldiers to confront the Prophet. Meanwhile Abu Sufyan changed his route and escaped. He told the Quraish to return, as he was safe. While most of them agreed to go back, Abu Jahl – a bitter enemy of Islam – insisted that they should teach Muslims a lesson; so that they do not intercept their caravans in future.

This was a serious turn as the Muslims numbered only three hundred while the Quraish were more than a thousand. This was the first battle for the Muslims. The Prophet was all the time busy praying to God. He said: "O Allah! Should this group (of Muslim) be defeated today, you will no longer be worshipped".[26]He continued to call out to Allah. Immediately the response came from Allah against the disbelievers.

I will assist you with one thousand angels, one after another
Al-Anfal: 8:9

Traditions mention that angels did appear and fight. The enemy gradually lost courage and soon Abu Jahl was killed. It was definitely a triumphant victory for the Muslims. Only fourteen Muslims were killed, while the enemy suffered a heavy loss of seventy people and an equal number were taken prisoners. The success in this war gave a new dimension to the military leadership of the Prophet and helped a large number of people to embrace Islam.

Battle Of Uhud
Shawwal 3 AH (March 625 AD)

There was a gap of less than two years between the battles of Badr and Uhud. It was not easy for the Quraish to digest their defeat; hence they started fresh preparations to launch a massive attack on the Muslims. They invited all the tribes to join together in their fight so as to crush the new Islamic State. They managed a force of three thousand people under the leadership of Abu Sufyan. The Muslims decided to resist the army outside the city of Madina near mountain Uhud. When the Prophet came close to the enemy, Abdullah bin Ubai, a hypocrite, rebelled against the Muslims. Along with him, one third of the army (about 300 people) was withdrawn.[27]

The Quraish were very cautious in attacking the enemy. Fierce fighting started in which Muslims lost many of their brave men. Hamza, the Prophet's uncle, fought with great bravery but was attacked by the enemy in darkness and killed. In spite of the great loss of Hamza and Mus'ab-bin-Umair, the Muslims were on their way to victory. The Prophet appointed archers on a position to block the enemy attacking from behind. When archers saw that enemy was retreating, many of them left their position and a part of the Meccan army attacked Muslims from behind and that turned the tables. It created a situation where the Prophet was about to be killed. The Muslims got entrapped. The Prophet was left with only nine members at the rear of the Army. This was a most unexpected situation, but the bravery of his companions was remarkable. They tried to shield the Prophet by taking all the attacks on themselves. One after the other, seven of them sacrificed their lives. At this critical stage, a woman companion by name Umm Ammarah shielded the Prophet with her body when the Qaniah got within striking distance of the Prophet and it was she who bore the brunt of the attacks. She suffered a dozen wounds and lost an arm. [28] This shows the unparalleled love and affection of the companions towards the Prophet.

The Prophet was badly injured. Anas narrated that the incisors of the Prophet were broken and his skull was also fractured. He was wiping out blood from his face. [29] In the meantime, a rumor was spread that the Prophet was killed. The Quraish decided to go back. But while going back they realized that the Prophet was still alive. Abu Sufyan shouted, "We will meet again at Badr, next year".

Battle Of Al-Ahzab (The Confederates)
5 AH (627 AD)

The battle of Uhud left a bad impression about the military credibility of the Muslims. This encouraged various Jewish tribes and hypocrites to come out openly against the Muslims. Bani Asad started making preparations for raid on Madina. The Prophet sent one hundred and fifty warriors under the command of Abu Salmah. They were taken by surprise and had to escape leaving behind their assets. After this, Bani Al-Nadeer plotted to kill Muhammad. They were ordered to leave their abode within ten days. Their gardens and other properties fell into the hands of the Muslims. The tribe of Bani Ghatfan also fled when the Prophet raided them.

Though the Prophet was able to curb the rebellious activities of these tribes, it was only a temporary phase. These tribes bore a grudge against the Muslims as they had been humiliated and the Muslims had seized their properties. They decided to join hands with the Quraish to attack the Muslims. The Quraish themselves were looking forward to an opportunity to take revenge. All of them united together and marched towards Madina. It was a force of ten thousand men and had it been a surprise attack, it would have been very difficult for Muslims to save themselves.

As the danger of attack was only from the northern side, the Prophet was advised to dig a trench on that side. It is believed that the work of digging the big trench was completed in six days. For the enemy, it was a new experience as they could not cross the trench and they were very upset. The only alternative left for them now was to incite Bani Qurizah, the Jewish tribe on the other side of Madina to rebel against the Muslims. As the Prophet had a treaty with them, he had not made defensive arrangements on that side. Although Bani Qurizah broke the treaty, they could not join the enemy due to the intelligent statesmanship of the Prophet. The siege was prolonged for more than twenty-five days. It was severe weather and the enemy was finding it very difficult. In the mean time, God's help came in the form of a severe windstorm. It was so intense that it was impossible for the enemy to stay there any more, so they left the battlefield.

The Treaty Of Al-Hudaibiyah
Dhul Qadah 6 AH (March 628 AD)

In the 6th year of Hijra, the Prophet saw in his dream that he was entering the sanctuary of Kabah. He took it as an order from God and started towards Mecca with fifteen hundred followers. When they reached Hudaibiyah, a place near Mecca, they got the news that the Quraish had decided to resist their mission. The Prophet did not want to fight with them so negotiations went on between the two parties. With great difficulty, the Quraish agreed to a peace treaty known as Al-Hudaibiyah. The Muslims were allowed to perform Umrah the next year only and permission was denied for this year. During the period of Umrah, they were allowed to stay in Mecca only for three days.

The Prophet's companions did not like the terms and conditions of the Treaty of Hudaibiyah. Even while drafting the treaty, the Quraish objected to the words 'Ar Rahman and Ar Rahim'and the 'Messenger of Allah'. The Prophet removed these words in the larger interest of the state. However, his companions were very upset and took it as an insult. They could not visualize the long-term interest of the treaty. One of the important conditions of the treaty was that all wars and hostilities would stop for a period of ten years. This was of great importance to the Muslims as they got some breathing time. For the past few years, their energies and resources were diverted towards war and preparations for war. The treaty proved to be a great triumph in the process of expansion of Islam. The three stalwart of Mecca, Amar bin Al-Aas, Khalid bin Al-Waleed and Uthman bin Talhah embraced Islam in the early 7th AH (628 AD).

The Battle Of Mu'tah
Jamada Al Ula 8 AH (Sept.629 AD)

In the post Hudaibiyah period also, there was no peace for the Prophet. There were sporadic invasions that were not very significant. However, the most forceful battle in the life of the Prophet was the battle of Mu'tah, which took place in 8 AH.The background of this battle was that the Prophet had sent a letter to the ruler of Busra, but the messenger was intercepted on the way and killed by Al-Ghassani, the Governor of Al-Balqa. This was considered to be a very serious crime and amounted to a declaration of war. The Prophet was very upset and ordered that an army of three thousand men be mobilized. The army was headed by Zayd bin Haritha, followed by Jaffar bin Abu Talib and Abdullah bin Rawaha. But the enemy was much more powerful. It could muster the strength of a hundred thousand troops and another additional army of the same size was to join them. This was a serious setback for the Muslims, as they never even imagined that they had to face such a big force. The Muslims fought with great courage, but lost their leaders one by one. Zayd was the first to be killed followed by Jafar and Abdullah. After the death of the three leaders, the people appointed Khalid bin Al-Waleed as the leader of the army. He was a brave fighter and used a different strategy. The Byzantines seeing this new strategy thought that they were entrapped. They stopped fighting. Taking advantage of this, the Muslims managed to retreat to

Madina. It was a miracle and it was with Allah's help that three thousand could fight against twenty thousand men. The total loss for the Muslims was not much, although they lost three of their brave leaders. It was the most significant and fierce battle during the lifetime of the Prophet.

The Conquest Of Mecca
20 Ramadan, 8 AH (10 January 630 AD)

The biggest victory for the Muslims was the conquest of Mecca in 8 AH. Mecca was conquered without any bloodshed. There was a background to this conflict. According to the treaty of Hudaibiyah, the Arab tribes were given the freedom to join either the Quraish or the Muslims. Consequently, Banu Bakr joined the Quraish and Banu Khuza joined the Muslims. They were prohibited from any aggressive act. However, after some time, hostilities began and Banu Bakr attacked Banu Khuza with the help of the Quraish. The hostilities amounted so much that they chased the people and massacred them in the premises of the Kabah, where no bloodshed was allowed. When Banu Khuza approached the Prophet for justice, the Quraish realized their mistake and sent Abu Sufyan to Madina for the renewal of the Treaty. However, the Prophet did not concede to their request.

The Muslims were eager to attack the Quraish. The Prophet proceeded towards Mecca on 10th of Ramadan with ten thousand people. On the way, when they reached Al-Juhfa, Al-Abbas bin Abdul Muttalib and his family came to join the Prophet. At Al-Abwa Abu Sufyan also came. Ali the son-in-law of the Prophet and a close companion, advised him to go to the Prophet and ask for pardon. Abu Sufyan recited some verses paying tribute to the Prophet and proclaiming Islam as the only religion. The Prophet granted him pardon and declared that whosoever takes refuge in Abu Sufyan's house is safe. The Prophet proceeded towards Kabah. Abu Sufyan was asked to go and warn the Quraish against any aggression. Abu Sufyan shouted at the helm of his voice, warning the Quraish. The Quraish realized their helplessness.

There was no opposition and the Mecca was conquered on the 20th Ramadan, The Prophet proceeded to knock down the idols. The Meccans realized the supremacy of Islam and started coming to embrace Islam. Never in the history of the world was a person able to conquer a city without shedding a drop of blood. This of course left a deep impression on other countries.

Ghazwa Hunain
Shawwal, 8 AH (January 630 AD)

The conquest of Mecca was a clear indication of the supremacy of the Muslims. However, in spite of this, there were some proud tribes suffering from a superiority complex, who were not prepared to accept the fate accompli. Under the leadership of Malik bin Awf An Nasri, they decided to attack the Muslims. On hearing this, the Prophet on 9th Shawwal, along with a force of more than 12 thousand Muslims, proceeded to face the enemy. They reached Hunain on 10th Shawwal.

The enemy's battalion started a fierce attack against the Muslims. The Muslims had to retreat in disorder and utter confusion. The Prophet prayed to Allah and said "O' Allah, send down your help". Later Muslims returned to the battle field and then the Prophet picked up a handful of sand and hurled it at the face of the enemy. Their eyes were thick with dust and the enemy began to retreat in confusion. Within a few hours they were badly defeated. The Quran has pointed this in Surah Al-Tauba, when it says

... On the Day of Hunain ... Allah sent down forces (angels)
which you saw not and punished the unbelievers ...
Al-Tauba: 9:25, 26

The Campaign of Tabuk
Rajab, 9AH (October 630 AD)

The invasion of Tabuk was the last in a long list of the military achievements of the Prophet. The Byzantine power, which was the greatest military force on earth at that time, was opposed to the Muslims. They always used to do something or the other to provoke the Muslims. The Prophet got the news that the Byzantines and the Ghassanide were making preparations for war with the Muslims. The people in Madina were alert all the time as they could be attacked any time. In view of this, the Prophet decided that the Muslims should stop Byzantines and fight a decisive battle. The Prophet marched toward Tabuk with an army of thirty thousand – the biggest army of the Muslims – but they did not have sufficient food and water and they had to starve many a time. [30]

When the enemy got the news of the Muslim army, they were so scared that they decided not to face it and thus no war took place. The whole process took fifty days, which was certainly a difficult time for the

Muslims. However, it established the supremacy of Muslims in the minds of their enemies. This war gave very good booty to the Muslims. It was reported that there were six thousand captives, twenty four thousand camels, forty thousand sheep and four thousand ounces of silver.

After the return of the Prophet from Tabuk, delegates of various tribes came to Madina to learn about Islam. The delegates arrived group after group as the Quran has described.

> *When there comes the help of Allah and victory, you see*
> *the people entering Allah's religion in multitudes.*
> *An-Nasr: 110:1, 2*

War Preparations

After establishing the Islamic State, the most challenging task before the Prophet was the organization and management of wars. In a period of ten years, he fought seven major and many minor wars. The period of wars extended from a few days to more than a month.

The preparation for war was a challenging task. It needed systematic and minute planning. Weapons had to be bought and a large number of camels were needed both for transportation as well as for food. Arrangements for stay and food had to be made. Nursing and care of the wounded and burial arrangements for the dead were also important aspects of war preparations. Apart from management skills, the preparation for war needed a lot of money. The public exchequer was not in a position to bear the heavy burden. Today, countries spend billions just on the maintenance of their defense forces; leave alone the question of an actual involvement in the war.

The heavy expenditure for wars in those days was mostly met by voluntary contributions. History is full of such examples when the Prophet's companions and others contributed a major proportion of their wealth. For instance, when the Prophet decided to invade Tabuk, contributions started pouring in from all directions. Abu Bakr gave away all his wealth, leaving nothing for his family. Umar parted with half of his fortune. Uthman, the Prophet's son-in-law gave two hundred ounces of gold and one thousand dinars. He also contributed nine hundred camels and a hundred horses.[31] Apart from this, there were small contributions from a number of people. Those who did not have money contributed their services. Hence, it was with the support of the people that the Prophet could win these wars successfully

The Prophet's Schedule of Work

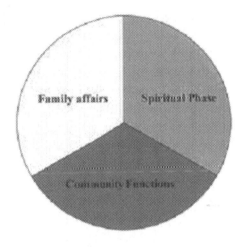

Time management is essential for any one who wishes to achieve something in life. There are thousands of people who aimlessly waste their whole life and have regrets in the end.The Prophet Muhammad(S) knew very well how best to utilize his time. He never wasted a single moment. He was always busy doing something concrete. He had broadly divided his day into three parts as follows:

1. His functions pertaining to the community.
2. Family affairs.
3. Spiritual phase and worship of Allah

The Functions Pertaining To The Community.

Every day from early morning until afternoon, he was busy in community work. His day started with the Morning Prayer. He was very particular about congregational prayers. He himself used to lead them. One day, an unusually large number of people were absent for the prayer. He was very angry and said "I wish I had appointed one of you to lead the prayer, and then I would venture outside to the homes of those absent and set their houses ablaze".[32]After prayers, there used to be long periods of learning and discussions. He would explain the meaning and implications of new verses as revealed to him. They exchanged news and views. The establishment of the Islamic State was not the end in itself; it was just the beginning of a long journey that the Muslim community had to make. There was peace inside Madina, but on the outskirts of the city, enemies of Islam had their own plans to crush the power of the new state. It was in these meetings that new strategies were worked out. The aim of the Prophet was to extend the boundaries of Islam as far and wide as possible, preferably not through war but by peaceful means. He was aware of the fact that the will and not the force is the basis of law.

Hence, in the last few years, his strategy was to win the love, affection and confidence of the people, particularly in the outlying areas of the state. One of the means that he adopted was matrimonial alliance, which proved to be the strongest bond.

Apart from working out the polices and programs for future actions, his time was spent in solving day-to-day practical problems of the people. People used to come to him from far and near, for solutions of their personal problems. Even large number of women used to come to him to know about Quran's interpretation concerning their specific problems.

He was an eloquent speaker. People used to enjoy listening to him for hours but he gave talks during peacetime only. During wars, he concentrated on strategies to secure victories.In Madina, lots of his time was taken up by wars.Fighting on the battlefield was one phase. However, there were many other aspects related to it. Preparation for major wars included arrangements for the boarding and lodging of thousands, supply of arms and ammunitions, logistics for the supply of food, water and care of the injured. The way these wars took place showed his systematic and skillful handling of all such problems. Even in the post-war period, there were a number of problems to be tackled such as the provision of medical facilities to the wounded, maintenance of the prisoners of war, looking after the families of those Muslims who were killed in wars, distribution of booty etc. These functions had to be performed skillfully and the Prophet excelled in that.

Family Affairs.

The second part of his work pertaining to his family has been discussed in the chapter The Prophet as a Husband.

The Spiritual Phase.

The spiritual phase of the Prophet started much before Prophethood. He was disturbed with the socio-religious conditions of Mecca. Unable to understand the mystery of the world, he would retreat to a cave named Hira and meditate. A few years after his marriage, it became his routine. He used to stay there for days together especially in the month of Ramadan. He started experiencing powerful inward signs. He said, "It was like the break of the light of dawn". Hence the Revelation, which came to him at the age of forty, was not all of a sudden. It was a gradual process preparing Muhammad for the great task ahead of him.

On his First Revelation, he was declared Messenger of Allah. God had chosen him to spread His message to the universe as a whole. It was obligatory for the Prophet to spend a lot of time in preparing for this job. Since, during the day, he was busy in disseminating knowledge, discussing and solving people's problems; nighttime was the best to concentrate on his spiritual work.

God himself had ordered the Prophet in Surah Muzzammal to observe night vigil in prayers.

O Muzzammil (folded in garments – one of which the nick names of the Prophet Muhammad)! Stand in prayers at night, but not the whole night, half of it or a little less or a little more, and recite the Quran with measured tone. Surely the getting up at night for prayer is most effective for controlling the self and most suitable for understanding the word's of Allah as well, because during the day you are hard-pressed with worldly affairs.
Al-Muzzammil: 73:1-7.

> **Surely your Lord knows that you stand in prayers nearly two-thirds of the night and sometimes one half or one third of it. He knows that you will not be able to keep it up so He has turned to you in mercy therefore read from the Quran as much as you easily can.**
> **Al-Muzzammil: 73:20**

It is believed that the first part of this Surah was revealed in the early days in Mecca. In the first seven verses, the Prophet had been commanded "Prepare yourself to shoulder the responsibilities of the great mission that has been entrusted to you, its practical form is that you should rise during the hours of night and stand up in prayer half the night, or for a little more or less of it devote yourself exclusively to Allah who is the owner of the whole universe". In the second section, which is believed to be revealed after ten years in Madina, the initial command that was given in the first section regarding night prayers was curtailed. It says, "offer as much of the **Tahajjud** prayers as you can."

From the very beginning, the Prophet had made it a point to spend the latter part of the night in prayers. His night prayers used to be very lengthy. Sometimes, his feet used to get swollen. Once Aisha pleaded with him: "O Messenger of Allah, why do you exert so much, when your Lord has forgiven all your sins?" The Prophet replied, "O Aisha, should I not become for that reason his most grateful servant?" It is believed that Gabriel used to come to the Prophet every year during Ramadan and he used to recite the whole Quran in his presence. During all the battles, the Prophet used to pray to God, requesting for help. God had always responded to his request, sending His aid for the Muslims to win the battles.

The New Islamic State

The establishment of the Islamic State brought a new dimension to world history. Within a short period of time, without bloodshed, Islam had crossed the boundaries of Arabia. The atmosphere everywhere was most congenial. When the Prophet was in Mecca, he was not allowed to perform his prayers freely. He was humiliated and tortured. Non-believers were after his life. The first thirteen years of Prophethood were years of great tension for all the believers. The way they were physically and mentally tortured was not only inhuman, but also unbelievable. For example, Bilal was a firm believer in Islam, but was a slave of Umayyah, the chief of Jumah, who was opposed to the new faith. He used to take Bilal out in the hot sun, pin him down to the ground with a large rock on his chest, and used to force him to either renounce Islam or die [33]. It was Abu Bakr who bought him and set him free. Abu Jahl was another wicked person who used to torture the new converts physically, financially and emotionally. Muhammad ibn Ibrahim al Tasmi narrated that when Uthman embraced Islam, his Uncle Hakam ibn Aias arrested him and tied him up with a rope.

God listened to the Muslims' prayers and things changed with the immigration to Madina. The Prophet did not go there because he was forced to do so. The people of Madina invited him. This was made possible by the Second Aqabah Pledge, which was concluded between the Prophet and the two important factions of the city of Madina - Aws and Khuzraj. The Prophet's authority was upheld both in religious and political matters.

The Mosque

When the Prophet entered Madina, his camel stopped at the place where the Mosque stands today. When the construction of the Mosque began, he not only personally supervised it but also actually participated in the work of construction by carrying bricks and other material. No King or Chief in history has ever participated in work of this manner. It provided not only a sense of involvement, and commitment to the labor but also the concept of dignity of labor of which we are proud of in the West.

The Mosque was constructed on a plot of 35 x 30 yards. [34] The Mosque was a very simple edifice. Not that they could not construct a grand building but the Prophet always avoided pomp and show and wanted to lead a very simple life. He desired that the building should be in the tradition of the one built by Moses. The Mosque remained unchanged during the lifetime of the Prophet except that its courtyard was enlarged to accommodate more people. In the beginning, there was no arrangement for light. There used to be bonfires for *Fajar* and *Isha* prayers. However, Tamim Dar introduced the concept of lamps. The Prophet said, "You have illuminated our Mosque, may God illuminate your life". [35]

Today, the pattern in construction of mosques has completely changed. They are not only big structured, but every attempt is made to make them beautiful and grand. Because of growing population and the need for a large number of people to participate in the multi-dimensional activities of the mosque, the size of a modern day mosque has to be large enough. However, it is not necessary to spend millions on the structure to make it beautiful.

The mosque has an important role to play in the life of an individual. It is not just a place for worship. It serves to unite the community, educate them and show them the right path. It helps in building a strong, dedicated and enlightened community. Women have an important role to play in the affairs of the Muslim community. Until recently, in many countries, the doors of the mosque were shut for women. Even now they are hardly involved in the affairs of the mosque. A woman, who shapes the family, has to be enlightened and hence special efforts have to be made to involve her in the affairs of the mosque.

For the betterment of the community and for presenting the correct image of Islam and Muslims to the world, the involvement of educated, and enlightened persons from different walks of life with broad vision is needed

Adhan

In Mecca, there was no place where congregational prayers could be performed. Non-believers, who always tried to humiliate and harm the believers, guarded the Kabah against the congregation of Muslims. The system of congregational prayers started only after the construction of the Mosque in Madina. However, the problem faced was, there was no method by which the people could be informed of the prayer timings. They used to assemble in the Mosque based on their own judgment of time. Many could not join due to the lack of information. The Prophet was worried about this lacuna. People suggested different ways, such as blowing of a conch or horn but the Prophet rejected both as they symbolized Christian and Jewish practices. One day, Abdullah ibn Zaid, one of the companions of the Prophet, saw in his dream a man wearing green clothes, standing on the roof of the mosque, putting two fingers into his ears and shouting a prayer call. The Prophet was very happy with this description. Concept of *Adhan* was introduced and the responsibility was entrusted to Bilal, who had a loud and pleasant voice.

Two Rakah obligatory prayers, in the morning and in the evening were established at an early period of Islam:

> ***Implore forgiveness for your sins and celebrate the
> prases of Your Lord, evening and morning
> Ghafir: 40:55***

The rule of five prayers a day was imposed after the Night journey of the Prophet

In the bignning Muslims used to turn their faces towards Jerusalem like Jews. After coming to Madina the relations between Jews and Muslims worsened in the meanwhile a Revelation came for the change of Qibla towards Allah's house With this change the Muslims were honored with the leadership of the world role (taken away from Bani Israel), and Prophet SAW's wish was fulfilled.In Mecca, recitation of the Quran was confined to the houses, in a feeble voice. But, Madina was like a heaven for the Muslims. From dawn to dusk, there were recitations of the Quran everywhere; in the houses, on the streets and in the Mosque. *Ahl-a Suffah's* main task was the recitation of the Quran. Almost throughout the day one could hear recitation of the Quran from the Mosque.

Every morning after the ***Fajar*** prayer, the Prophet used to address the gathering, explain the Quranic verses and discuss with the people the day-to-day problems facing the community and tried to work out strategies. Everything was done with mutual consent of the people and not by imposing decisions on them. That was the democratic spirit that the Prophet introduced in Madina, in contrast to the dictatorship that had been practiced earlier. Islam was now firmly established. Revelations prescribed the giving of alms and fasting during Ramadan. The concept of Haram and Halal was also established.

In order to stabilize the situation, the first thing the Prophet did was to frame the Constitution for the new state. The Constitution, which was called *Sahifah*, reveals the great statesmanship and vision of the Prophet. It is believed that the Prophet himself had dictated the provisions of this document. The Major factions in the city ratified the Constitution. The parties to the covenant were the Prophet on one side and the three major factions, viz., the Mahajirun (Immigrants), the Ansar (the residents of Madina) and the various clans and tribes of the Jews of Madina. [37] The *Sahifa*h laid down the foundation for the new Islamic state on a solid legal basis. Law enforcement was a collective responsibility. Although an Islamic State, it gave the freedom of religion to other citizens

Socio-Economic Problems Of Immigrants

The Prophet along with a large number of his followers had migrated to Madina and this flow continued for quite some time. The biggest problem of the immigrants was of socio-economic nature, as they were without homes and any means of livelihood. It was the Prophet's vision that helped to solve this problem in a most simple but practical way. Each immigrant was assigned to one Ansar, who was made responsible for the settlement of the immigrant. Most of the Ansars were so committed and enthused that they were prepared to share their houses, their property and everything with their immigrant brothers. This was not only a short-term arrangement but had far reaching implications on their whole lives. There was another problem of the large number of poor and destitute who could not be accommodated anywhere. They used to live in the Mosque and the Prophet and the community at large looked after their needs.

Today, there are thousands of Muslims, from all over the worlds, which are forced to migrate and take shelter in other countries. Although the local governments try to rehabilitate them, but the Muslim community, is largely found lacking in the spirit of the Ansar. Muslims are in majority in 56 countries some of these countries are quite rich in natural resources and financially well off. But they have no such set up as could be mobilized for the support of such grants. There is an urgent need to give a serious thought to this question especially in view of recent war-like climate in Muslim countries that have made a large number of Muslims refugees.

Human Relations

The secret of the Prophet's success lies in his excellence in human relations. Those who came into contact with him with, the exception of his declared enemies became so enamored by his personality that they would gladly sacrifice their wealth, health and happiness for him. History is full of incidents that reveal the uncanny love and affection they entertained for him. His charming personality, his treatment, behavior and concern for everyone brought him closer to every heart. Every one used to get the impression that he or she had a special place in the Prophet's heart.

Abu Bakr was his closest friend. He was very sincere, honest and devoted. He accompanied the Prophet from the beginning, till the end. He sacrificed everything for the sake of the Prophet. He was the person who had given all of his wealth, keeping nothing for his own family when the Prophet was collecting donations for the preparation of a war. He made all arrangements for the Prophet's migration to Madina and accompanied him on the hazardous trip too. Abu Bakr's devotion and love for the Prophet could be judged from one single incident. During the battle of Uhud, his eldest son Abdullah, who had not embraced Islam, challenged the Prophet, Abu Bakr took out his sword and was about to attack him, but the Prophet saved the situation.[38]

Umar bin Khattab was also one of the most trusted aides after embracing Islam. He was such a formidable person that his very presence scared away the enemies of Islam. He was always concerned about the comfort and welfare of the Prophet. One day, he burst into tears when he found the Prophet lying on a mattress that had left its marks on his body. When the Prophet asked him why he was crying, he said, "I thought of Caesar and Chosroes sitting on thrones of gold, wearing silk and you, the Messenger of Allah, are lying uncomfortably on this simple mattress"[39]. Umar also donated a huge part of his wealth for war preparations. Uthman, the

Prophet's son-in-law, was another very devoted person. He gave away most of his assets in the cause of the new faith. The Prophet always had great affection and respect for him. After the death of his daughter Ruqayya, he got his other daughter Umm Kulthum married to him. Once, he remarked that if he had forty daughters, he would have married them to Uthman one by one. Ali bin Abu Talib was his cousin and son-in-law, but he always treated him like his own son. Ali was always with the Prophet. He took part in practically all the wars. Ali was most obedient and had great love and respect for the Prophet. When the Prophet was migrating to Madina, enemies who wanted to kill him surrounded his house. Gabriel warned him not to sleep in his bed. The Prophet asked Ali to sleep in his bed, Ali, knowing the risk obeyed him.

The Prophet always maintained good relations with all his relatives, even though some of them, like his uncle Abu Lahab, had tortured him a lot. However, he never thought of taking revenge. He left everything to God. He had immense love for his uncle Abu Talib who protected him for forty years, despite the fact that he himself had not accepted Islam. The Prophet was loved so much by his relatives that even though many of them had not accepted his religion, all of them willingly went through the great hardship of socio-economic boycott of the family by the Quraish for three long years. His love for his first wife Khadijah was so great that even after her death he used to maintain good relations with her sister Halah and her friends. Whenever he used to sacrifice any animal, he was very particular to send meat to Khadijah's friends. He frequently used to visit all his relations and spend time with them.

The Prophet never differentiated between the rich and poor, between master and the servant. He treated all equally, irrespective of their status. His behavior with slaves and servants was remarkable. He always treated them with respect. Khadijah's slave Maysarah [40], who accompanied the Prophet on Khadijah's trade mission, was very much impressed by his behavior. Khadijah was influnced by his praise, which ultimately led to her marriage with Muhammad.

Zayd was a slave boy who was presented to him by his wife Khadijah after their marriage. The Prophet loved him so much that Zayd preferred to stay with him rather than to go back to his own father. Impressed by this devotion, the Prophet declared him to be his adopted son, before his Prophethood. Throughout his life, Zayd was loyal to the Prophet. He had great attachment to the Prophet. The Prophet's words were law for him. Once the Prophet remarked about Umm Ayman (his caretaker from his childhood), "He that would marry a woman of the people of paradise, let him marry Umm Ayman". Zayd took this remark to heart and married her, though she was a widow with a child and at least twenty years older than him. She continued to be his wife till the end, though on the advice of the Prophet he also married Zaynab bint Jahsh, but divorced her within a year.

The Prophet had many special relationships in his life that were not shared by anyone except him and the person in question. One of these was with Umm Ayman [41]. Many a time he used to call her "Mother" and she was always treated as a part of his family.

The Prophet had great respect and love for his foster mother Halima. Whenever she was in difficulty, the Prophet and Khadijah used to help her. Once when there was a widespread drought, Khadijah made a gift of forty sheeps and a howdah camel to her.[42] After the battle of Hunain, when the Prophet left for Tai'f, to face the defeated idolaters, an elderly woman captive, Shayma came forward to claim herself as the foster sister of the Prophet. After recognizing that she was the daughter of Halima, he not only released her, but also gave her a big share of the booty.[43] The Prophet always welcomed his companions and friends not only in the Mosque but also in his apartment. He used to share his meager meals with them. They felt so comfortable and at home that they would linger on in his house for a long time, not realizing the inconvenience caused to the Prophet. It was on the occasion of the Prophet's marriage to Zaynab bint Jahsh, when his companions stayed for a long time after dinner, that God revealed an Ayah to remind the people of their limitation.

Do not enter the house of the Prophet without permission, nor stay waiting for meal time; but if you are invited to a meal, enter, when you have eaten, disperse and do not seek long conversation. As such behavior annoys the Prophet, he feels shy in asking you to leave, but Allah doesnot feel shy in telling the truth.
Al Ahzab: 33: 53

He was very particular in maintaining good relations with his neighbors. He used to say, "He will not enter paradise, whose neighbor is not secure from his wrong conduct". He also used to say "Show mercy to people on earth so that Allah will have mercy on you in heaven"[44] Not only did he maintain good relations with neighbors, but was also particular that his wives do the same. He never used to turn down invitations of his friends and neighbors. He instructed his wives to send gifts whenever possible to the neighbors, even if they belonged to a different faith. Once Aisha had only a small piece of meat, which was sufficient only for one neighbor, so she asked to whom she should send it. The Prophet replied "the one nearest to you".

He used to attach much importance to human sentiments and values. Once, after victory at Khyber, when Bilal brought two young slave girls, Safiyah and her cousin through the place where the dead bodies of their relatives were lying. The Prophet told him, "You should not have brought them by this route". After the victory of the battle of Hunain, there were a large number of captives including women and children, most of them were poorly clad. The Prophet ordered new garments for all of them.

His relations with his wives are discussed in detail in the chapter 'The Prophet as a Husband'. Suffice it to say that he treated them as his equals and never tried to dominate them. He was so affectionate and friendly with his children and grandchildren that they never felt the generation gap. On seeing his youngest daughter Fatima, he used to stand up and kiss her.

The above-mentioned incidents epitomize his exemplary approach to human relations. He was accessible to everyone. He always met them with an open heart. Love begets love. It was his love for the people that caused them to reciprocate with abundant love. There is no example in world history where people were prepared to sacrifice every thing for the sake of their leader. It is perhaps due to this reason that Michael Hart has ranked him as the most influtional single figure in human history.[45]

The End Of An Era

The Prophet's Stay In Mecca And Madina

1.	Prophet's Span of Life	63 years
2.	Total Stay In Mecca	53 years
3.	Period of Prophethood In Mecca	13 Years
4.	Prophet's Stay In Madina	10 Years

After laying down the foundation of a strong Islamic State the Prophet started feeling that his job in this world was over. When in the 10th year of Hijra, he sent his companion Muadh to Yemen, he told him "May be you will not see me after this year, on your way back, you may pass by my mosque and grave".[46] He also had some other indications. For example every year in Ramadan Gabriel, used to come to him to review the recitation of Quran by him, but he came twice during the last year of his life. He told his daughter, Fatima, that his time on earth is perhaps comming to an end.

In the same year he had the intution of going to Haj. On hearing this news, people started joining him in great numbers.[47]All his wives accompanied him. Abu Bakr accompanied him with his pregnant wife Asma bint Umays who gave birth to a son on the way that was named Muhammad

On reaching Mecca, he prayed to God to increase Kabah's honor and magnification, bounty and reverence and piety that it received from mankind.[48] After performing the rituals on 9th Dhul-Hijjah, he addressed the gathering. His address is known as *Khutba al-Hajat- ul Wada* or his farewell address. It was a historic event.

'O' people! Listen to what I say. I do not know whether I will ever meet you at this place once again after this year. It is unlawful for you to shed the blood of one another or take (unlawfully) the fortunes of one another … Behold all practices of paganism and ignorance are now under my feet … usury is forbidden. O people! Fear Allah concerning women … it is incumbent upon them to honor their conjugal rights and not to commit acts of impropriety. Verily I have left amongst you the Book of Allah and the Sunnah of His Messenger, which if you hold fast, you shall never go astray. [49]

As soon as he completed his address, Surah Al-Maidah was revealed.

…..Today I have perfected your religion for you and I have completed My favour upon you. I have approved of Islam as your religion.
Al-Maidah: 5: 3

On hearing this, Abu Bakr burst into tears and realized that Prophet's time was over. When the Prophet returned from his visit to Al Baquia on the 29th of Safar, 10AH, (5th June 631AD) he complained of a severe headache, one that he had never suffered in his life. However, even then he went to the Mosque and after leading the prayer, said, "There is a slave amongst the slaves of God unto whom God has given the choice between this world and that which is with God, and the slave has chosen that which is with God." On hearing this, Abu Bakr started weeping. He knew that the servant was no one other than the Prophet himself.

From the Mosque, the Prophet went to his wife Maymunah, who had her turn that day. Then he went to Aisha's apartment, to inform her of his suffering. He found that Aisha too had severe headache. Aisha became alarmed on seeing him. He tried his best to go to the Mosque and lead the prayer. But his illness increased. When he was in one of his wives' apartment, he asked her where he would be going next. The wives realized that he was keen to go to Aisha's apartment, so they decided to give their turn to Aisha. Most of the time he was resting his head on Aisha's lap. His all other wives were also with him.

Five days before his death, the Prophet's temperature rose very high. He asked his wives to pour seven pots of water brought from different wells over him. After this, he went to the Mosque and addressed the people. He warned them "Do not make my tomb a worshipped idol".[50] When he became very weak, he could not lead the prayers, and so he asked Abu Bakr to lead the prayers. This was an indication that Abu Bakr would take his place, although there was a group of people who were expecting Ali to be his successor.

One day, before his death, he freed his slaves and distributed seven dinars that were in his possession, in charity. He was sixty-three years old when he breathed his last on 12th Rabi ul Awal 10 AH (18th June 631 AD). Umar was in a state of shock. He could not believe that the Prophet had died. He was still trying to convince people that the Prophet's condition was good. Abu Bakr broke the news to the people. He recited the following verses that were revealed after the battle of Uhud. [51]

> *Muhammad is but a messenger and messengers have passed away before him. If he dies or be slain, well ye then turn upon your heels? Whose turneth upon his heels will thereby do not hurt unto, God will reward the thankful.*
> *Al-Imran: 3:144*

After hearing this Surah, the people realized its hidden meaning and significance.

There was some confusion on the question of his burial. Some suggested that he should be buried along with his daughters and son Ibrahim. However, Abu Bakr remembered the saying of the Prophet that 'No Prophet dieth but is buried where he died'. So they decided to bury him in Aisha's apartment where he had breathed his last. All the people of Madina wanted to pay their homage to him. They offered prayers. Late in the evening, he was laid to rest into his grave by Ali and others.

The Prophet had already warned the Muslims not to use his grave as a shrine to be glorified, because that was shirk and prohibited. It is permissible to visit his grave and send Salam to him and seek forgiveness for ourselves but what is forbidden in Islam is to call on the Prophet after he has died and ask him to help us in our difficulties.[52] Thus came the end of his physical life rather it marked the beginning of a new and pulsating life of his teachings.

The Prophet's Personality

Personality is a very complex word. It includes not merely physique but an aggregate of all other attributes - behavior, temperament, emotion and mental faculties that make a unique individual. In the case of Prophet Muhammad(S) it is not only difficult but also perhaps impossible to describe him in accurate terms. No picture could be comprehensive enough to capture his multidimensional personality.

As per the narration of Ibn-Kathir, it is believed that the Prophet was a very handsome person. His father Abdullah was considered the Yusuf (Joseph) of his time. His grandfather Abdul Muttalib was also a very handsome person. The Prophet was of medium height, with an unusually large head and with a sharp nose. He had black, slightly curly hair and a black beard. He had exceptionally white teeth. He had the habit of brushing his teeth before every prayer.

The most striking aspects were his black eyes and his bright white complexion with a reddish tan. His face was the index of his mind. It reflected his love for God, piety, honesty, sincerity, his concern for every one and above all his intelligence. Some used to call him a full moon; others describe him as a rising sun.

It is narrated by Hasan bin Ali that once he asked his uncle, Hind bin Ab Haalah to tell him about the way Prophet talked, and he said "He was reserved in speech and did not talk unnecessarily. His speech was very clear from the beginning till the end. He was polite and never harsh or insulting to the person addressed. He used to enquire into the needs of his companions and other people and tried his best to help them. He was close to the people. He did not alienate from them. He paid attention to every person of the gathering, every one considered himself to be nearest to the Prophet. He was always cheerful, polite and gentle. He was never rude or harsh."[54] His character was spotless. Allah Himself has praised his character and stated that his character was noble and unequalled.

You are indeed on an exalted standard of character and morals.
Al Qalam: 68:4

Aisha had remarked about his manners. She said, his manners were as described in the Quran.On the authority of Urwah, Aisha is reported to have said, "None was better than the Prophet in morals. Whenever any one called him, he would hasten to him saying *'Labaik'*. It was for this reason that in the Quran, Allah had declared thus.[53]

Verily thou art on the best moral pattern
Al-Qalam: 68:4

The Prophet was a perfect example of a man who lived a very simple life.He used to wear very simple clothes, though spotlessly clean. His dwelling was a hut with walls of unbaked clay and a thatched roof of palm leaves covered by camel skin. He was very gentle and kind hearted, always gracious and overlooking to faults of others. He always received people with courtesy and showed respect to older people and said "to honour old men is to show respect to Allah." He used to visit poorest of ailing person and adviced all people to do the same. (Bukhari-Sahih Bukhari.)

Once the Prophet had said about himself that "Allah has sent me as an apostle, so that I may demonstrate perfection of character, refinement of manners and loftiness of deportment."He was against the concept of superiority based on race, color, family etc and said "righteousness alone was the criteria of ones superiority over others".Once during the journey when the food was being cooked he started collecting firewood. His companions requested him not to do so but he replied "I do not like to attribute any distinction to myself.Allah does not like the man who consider himself superior to his companions."

Even when the Prophet won the wars he was never boastful.He was always magnanimous and greatful to Allah.When he conquered Mecca and entered the city- whose people tourtured, mocked and reviled him- he entered with his head bowed and granted clemency to his inhabitants.

Aisha has narrated about his temperament when she says, "the Messenger of Allah never beat any servant or any woman or anyone else". She further says, "He was never ill-tempered, nor had an abusive tongue.

He did not return evil for evil but forgave and overlooked the shortcomings of others". [55]

The Prophet never bothered about worldly pleasures. It is unimaginable to think that the head of the state would go without food for days together. Abu Hurairah narrated that once when he visited the Prophet, he was performing *salat* in a sitting position. He asked the reason and the Prophet's reply was "hunger". Abu Talha had narrated that once they complained to the Prophet about their hunger. On hearing this, the Prophet exposed his belly on which two stones were tied because of his hunger.[56] Today's readers may be surprised on hearing these stories and may ask why the Prophet and his family had to starve when he was the head of the state and used to get good bounties in wars. The main reason was his generosity. He used to distribute everything among the poor and the needy, keeping nothing for himself or his family. Even his wives were very generous. Most of them used to distribute the entire amount that they used to get for their expenses. The Prophet was not in the habit of saying no to any needy person. If he did not have the money, he would take a loan to meet their needs.

It is beyond doubt that he had a very magnetic personality. Whenever anyone used to come into contact with him he would get mesmerized by his personality. If we only look back and throw a glance at his close associates– Abu Bakr, Umar, Ali, Uthman, Zayd, Umm Ayman – just to mention a few. It is clear that the type of love and affection and a sense of sacrifice that they had shown were never recorded in history for any other individual. All his wives were deeply in love with him, even though in many cases there was a difference in age of 30 to 40 years. His Jewish wife Safiyah who was just 17 years old at the time of her marriage had set an example of deep love for the Prophet. A girl whose father, brother, and husband were killed in the war by Muslims was so much impressed by the personality of the Prophet that she immediately agreed to be his wife.

One of the greatest qualities of the Prophet was his trust in Allah. In a period of 23 years of prophethood, he demonstrated blind faith and trust in Allah. He underwent serious threats to his life. During the social boycott Quraish were after his life but he continued to go to Kabah to pray. In many wars he was at the edge of defeat but he never lost his trust in Allah and continued to pray for success. Allah always rewarded him for his trust. Once a Jew woman mixed poison in his food. He spit it out after taking a morsel, though one of his disciples who ate it died next day. When that woman was brought before him she admitted that she wanted to kill him.

The Prophet said "Allah would not have allowed you to do that" and he did not take revenge from her. Today even though we believe in Allah we do not have that blind faith and trust in Him. In the time of distress we try to look to other sources for help which amounts to *shirk*.

Another great quality of the Prophet was his tolerance. He knew how to control his emotions. He never acted violently when his enemies humiliated him. History is full of such instances [57] He could have reacted violently, abused them or fought with them, but he did nothing of this sort. He kept on praying. Even when he was angry with his wives, he never abused them, nor scolded them. He preferred to be quiet and did not talk to them for some time.

He was a great statesman and always looked towards ultimate goal. He was prepared to compromise on things coming in the way of achieving his objective. The best example was the treaty of Hudaibiyah, which proved to be a great landmark in the process of peace making.[58]Another example of his tolerance was the incident when a villager entered the Mosque and started urinating. The Prophet's companions shouted at him "stop, stop". However, the Prophet said, "Don't stop his urination". Then he called the person and explained the significance of the mosque and then asked someone to pour a bucket of water to clean it.[59] Had this occurred today, people would have turned violent and not only killed that person but would have made an issue out of it, destroying peace in the society. However, the Prophet was very pragmatic person and knew how to solve a problem without inciting the emotions of the people.

The Prophet did not take revenge even against his enemies. Abu Sufyan was a bitter enemy of Islam, but when he surrendered and accepted Islam, the Prophet dealt with him respectfully. He announced, "Whosoever enters the house of Abu Sufyan will be safe". [60]On the day of the victory of Mecca, when Sufyan bin Harb Al-Hrith bin Hisham and Sufwan bin Umaiyah came to the Prophet, Umar told the Prophet "Now Allah has given you power over them. I will remind you of all their deeds which they did with us". However, the Prophet said, "I will say to you what Yusuf (Joseph) had said to his brothers. This day let no reproach be (cast) on you. May Allah forgive you. He is most Merciful to those who show mercy". (Yousuf XII: 92)

The Prophet was kind not only to human beings but also to animals. He forbade the practice of cutting tails and manse of horses, of branding animals at any soft spot and keeping horses saddled unnecessary. If he used to see any animal over loaded or ill fed he would say to the owner "Fear

Allah in your treatment to animals." Once while on a journey someone picked up some bird's eggs, the bird was upset, the Prophet asked the person to replace them immediately. While marching towards Mecca they passed a female dog with puppies. The Prophet ordered that they should not be disturbed. He said there is heavenly reward for every act of kindness done to animal.

It is most unfortunate that in today's society, people have neither the patience nor the required vision. They become emotional over small things and react in a most violent way – abusing people, doing revengeful deeds – even to the extent of killing innocent persons who may be in no way connected with the incident. The irony is that they neither understand the Quran correctly nor the essence of the teaching of the Prophet. The reading of the Quran and praying of *salat* only do not make a person a true Muslim. His character should portray him as Muslim. By acting violently they only tarnish the image of Islam and give a chance to other communities to exploit their follies. Islam is not a religion of retaliation. It gives the message of love and peace for humanity as a whole. Unless Muslims realize and practice the essence of teaching of Islam, they would continue to harm their own interests.

References and Note

1. Abdul Muttalib in the beginning had only one son, then he vowed to God. God gave him 10 sons, the youngest was Abdullah. After a gap of more than twenty years, he had at least two more sons, Abbas, who was three years older to Muhammad and Hamza who was a few months younger to him.

2. Safi-ur-Rehman Mubarakpuri: AR Raheeq Al Makhtum (The Sealed Nectar), Biography of the Noble Prophet, Maktaba Darus Salam 1995, p. 52.

3. Martin Lings: Muhammad – His life based on the earliest sources: Suhail Academy Lahore, Pakistan, Third Ed 1987, p. 17.

4. Ibid, p. 20.
   They are great variations in the number. It varies from 30,000 to 100,000.

5. There is a difference of opinion on the exact date of birth of the Prophet. While most of the writers agree on 12th Rabi-ul –Awal, the Egyptian astronomer, Mohammed Pasha Falki has written a treatise on the Prophet's date of birth and has proved that it was 9th Rabi-ul-Awal (20th April 571) Quoted by Shibli Numani, Sirat- un-Nabi, Vol I, Islamic Book Service. New Delhi 1998, p. 153.

6. Mubarakpuri, op. cit., p.58.

7. Martin Lings, op. cit., p. 26.

8. While most of the writers such as Shibli Numani and Martin Lings have mentioned that Muhammad was brought back to Mecca by his servant girl Barkha (Umm Ayman) Safi -Ur-Rahman Mubarakpuri mentioned that he was accompanied by his grandfather, Abdul Muttalib (Mubarakpuri, op. cit., p 59).

9. Martin Lings, op. cit., p. 30

10. Mubarakpuri, op. cit., p. 62.

11. Martin Lings, op. cit., p. 33.

12. Mubarakpuri, op. cit., p. 64.

13. Ibid, p. 44.

14. Zakaria Bashier, Makkan Crucible: The Islamic Foundation Revised Ed. 1991, pp. 99, 101. Also Mubarakpuri op. cit.pp 70,71

15. Zakaria Bashier, Makkan Crucible, op. cit., p. 106.
16. Mubarakpuri, op. cit., p. 105.
17. There is difference of opinion on the dates of the deaths of the two. Some believe tha Khadijah died first. But the traditions are in favor of the second opinion that Khadijah followed Abu Talib. Both the deaths took place in a span of a few weeks in 619 AD.
18. Yusuf Kandhlawi,Maulana Mohammad: Hayatus Sahabah (The lives of the Sahabah) translated by Dr. Majid Ali Khan, Idara Ishaat-e-Diniyat, New Delhi, Second Ed.1989. Vol I, p. 316.
19. Ibid p. 322.
20. Ibid p. 328.
21. Ibid p. 330.
22. Mubarakpuri op. cit. p. 140
23. a) Ibid p.138.
    b) Javeed Akhter —Seven Phases of Prophet Muhammad's(S) life. Publisher -ISPI
24. Ibn Hashim1/399 quoted by Mubarkpuri, op. cit., p. 151.
25. There is a difference of opinion on the question of how many days the Prophet stayed in Quba. The majority of writers are of the opinion that he stayed there for four days. However, Urwah ibn Zubair narrates that he stayed there for more than ten nights (Yusuf Kandhlawi op. cit., p. 424) whereas Shibli Naumani claims that he stayed for fourteen days (Sirat-un-Nabi, vol. I, p. 250).
26. Mubarakpuri, op. cit. p. 220.
27. Ibid p. 250.
28. Mahmood Ahmad Ghadanfar: Great Women of Islam, Darussalalm, Riyat, 2001, p. 12.
29. Yusuf Kandhlawi, Hayatus Sahabah vol. I op.cit. p 334
30. Mubarkpuri, op. cit p.427
31. Yusuf Kandhlawi op. cit. vol 1 p 426
32. Ibid, Vol III, p. 136.
33. Yusuf Kandhlawi op. cit. p 346. Martin Lings op. cit. p. 79.
34. Zakaria Bashier: Sunshine at Madina, The Islamic Foundation, 1990, p. 50.
35. Ibid p. 55.
36. Yusuf Kandhalwi, op.cit.vol III p.129.
37. Zakaria Bashier Sunshine at Madina op. cit. p. 85
38. Martin Lings, op. cit., p. 184.

39. Afrog Hasan, Azwaj -e- Mutahharath. Islamic Book Foundation, New Delhi, Vol. I, 1996, p. 44.

40. Maysarah was Khadijah's servant who accompanied Muhammad on a business trip before their marriage.

41. Martin Lings, op. cit.p., 164

42. Ibid, p. 39.

43. Mubarkpuri, op. cit. p. 408.

44. Ibid, pp. 190, 193.

45. Michael H.Hart, The 100 A Ranking of the Most Influential Persons in History. A citadel Press Book Published by Carol Publishing Group, USA, 1978, Ed. 1992.

46. Salem Foad B, The Serah of Prophet Muhammad(S), Ventage Press, New York, 2001, p. 310.

47. Martin Lings, op. cit., p. 332.

48. Ibid, p. 333.

49. Mubarakpuri, op. cit., p. 463.

50. Muata Imam Malik quoted by Mubarakpuri op. cit, p. 47.

51. Martin Lings, op. cit., p. 342.

52. Salem Foad, op. cit., p. 334.

53. Yusuf Kandhlawi, Vol II, op. cit., pp. 582, 583.

54. Ibid, Vol. I.

55. Ibid, Vol. II, pp. 586-587

56. Ibid, Vol I, p. 373.

57. Please refer to the chapter on Prophet hood.

58. Please refer to the chapter – Prophet in the Battlefield

59. Yusuf Kandhlawi, op. cit., Vol. 3, p. 118.

60. Mubarakpuri op cit p 392

Part II

The Prophet With His Family

Prophet's family in Mecca before Khadijah's death

Wives	Daughters	Son In Law
Khadijah	Zaynab	Abu al-Aas
	Ruqayya	Uthman ibn Affan
	Umm Kulthum	
	Fatima	

Prophet's Family In Madina at the time of his death

Wives	Daughters	Son In Law	Grand Children
Sawda	Fatima	Ali bin Abu Talib	Ummamah
Aisha			Hasan
Hafsah			Hussain
Umm Salamah			Kulthum
Zaynab Jahsh			Zaynab
Juwayriah			
Umm Habiba			
Safiya			
Maymunah			

The Prophet With His Family

The Quran is not merely a religious book. It is a guide for the establishment of a just social order. The Quranic laws cover many aspect of social and family life. It goes into detail in prescribing the relationships between different segments of society. It attaches great importance to the concept of family, which is the basic unit of every society. If the foundation of a family is not laid on a strong footing, the whole society may collapse. This is the message given by the Quran and the Prophet. However, modern society has shifted the emphasis from the family to the individual. Right from childhood, the child is taught 'mine' and not 'our', which is contrary to the teaching of Islam. This is the tragedy of the civilized society of today.

Prophet Muhammad(S) attached great importance to the concept of family, despite the fact that he was the only child of his parents and did not cherish the company of his siblings. He could not even enjoy the affection of his father, since he died before his birth. He lived with his mother for hardly two to three years followed by his stay at the extended family of his grandfather. Abdul Muttalib had more than ten sons and five daughters. His uncle Abu Talib also had ten children. With uncle, aunt and their several children, the Prophet had a very large extended family and there was great love and affection among them. He was very close to his uncle, Abbas, who was only three years older than him and also Hamza, who was his uncle as well as his cousin and was a few months younger than him. He was also very intimate with the children of Abu Talib, in whose house he was brought up. In this extended family, he learnt caring and sharing, which was his message to humanity throughout his life.

In Mecca, after his marriage with Khadijah, his family consisted of his wife and children. He had two sons and four daughters. However, only the daughters survived but three of them died during his lifetime. Only Fatima survived, and died a few months after the Prophet's death. He loved his daughters and grand children very much.

His household also included Ali bin Abu Talib, who was brought up by him, and Zayd, who was his adopted son. Although, after his Prophethood, he had a very trying life due to the constant opposition and harassment of the Quraish, but at home, he had a peaceful life. The credit goes mainly to the great lady, Khadijah, who had great understanding, tolerance and patience, made sacrifices and was an embodiment of love and affection. Support from his family gave him the courage to face all the hardship and tortures he was subjected to by his enemies.

His family life, after the death of Khadijah, and especially after his marriages in Madina, was a bit different. He did not have the same peaceful atmosphere at home, which he used to have in Mecca. With several wives, it was not easy to maintain a balance, although he always tried to be fair and just. In an ordinary family even just two wives are rarely found on talking terms. The Prophet succeeded in effecting a harmonious atmosphere at his home. Every evening, the Prophet along with all his wives used to meet at one place. They used to chat and sometimes discuss different issues. There was, of course jealousy among the wives, but he always tried to keep it down to the minimum. All his nine wives were present at the time of his death.

Some Observations About
the Prophet's Marriages

Prophet Muhammad(S) was adored and loved by thousands of people and was considered to be the most influential man in world history. It was difficult to find any flaw in his message, hence his critics had to search for some other ground for attack. They focused their attention on his personal life. The attacks were mostly on three aspects:

1. His multiple marriages.
2. His marriage with Aisha, when she was only six or seven years old.
3. His marriage with Zaynab bint Jahsh – the divorced wife of his adopted son, Zayd.

A close examination of the facts reveals that none of the objections raised by the critics is valid

Multiple Marriages

History has to be understood in the relevant perspective. To judge the past with the present day norms leads one to incorrect conclusions. It is a fact that the Prophet had several wives. When he died, he left nine widows[1] while two had already died in his lifetime. The concept of multiple wives was not new. Even among the Prophets, some had many wives. Prophet Abraham had two wives, Prophet Yaqub had four wives, Prophet David had numerous wives and Prophet Solomon had numerous wives and three hundred concubines.[2] Even the Prophet's gtrandfather Abdul Muttalib had at least three wives, Abu Bakr and Umar had two or more wives.

In ancient times, polygamy had become a necessity since there were frequent wars resulting in a large number of widows and orphans. In the absence of any institutional arrangement, their responsibility had to be shared by society. The Quran in Surah An-Nisa has indicated a preference for marrying widows in order to take care of the orphans.

In the pre-Islamic society of Arabs, polygamy was the order of the day. In fact, a person used to have ten to twelve wives.[3] Sexual relations were not always governed by the institution of marriage. It was in this background that Surah Nisa was revealed:

> *If ye fear that ye shall not be able to deal justly with the orphans,*
> *Marry women of your choice, Two or three or four; but if ye*
> *fear that ye shall not be able to deal justly (with them), then*
> *only one, or (a captive) that your right hands possess, that*
> *will be more suitable, to prevent you from doing injustice.*
> *An-Nisa: 4:3*

Viewed in the proper context, it is clear that the Quran did not give a free license for having up to four wives; rather it was a restriction on the prevailing practice to cut down the maximum number to four. A close examination reveals that the wordings of the Surah leaned towards monogamy.

The question then arises, why did the Prophet marry several wives? The answer to this question is found partly in the verses revealed by God and partly in the socio-political conditions of that time. For this purpose, the life span of the Prophet may be divided into two parts - the first part from the age of 25 to 50 years and the second part from the age of 51 to 63 years.

In the first phase of twenty-five years, he had only one wife. He had other wives only after the death of Khadijah and especially after migrating to Madina when his age was more than fifty years. The allegation of his critics that he was a lover of women and had over-riding sexual desires appears baseless against this background. In the first fifty years of his life, there was not a single incident that supported such a point of view. Right from his youth, he was a different person and never indulged in sexual aberrations that normally attract a young person. Had he any such desire, he would have married young and beautiful girls. On the contrary, his first wife was a woman twice marriede, having children and fifteen years older than him. The criticism that he had married Khadijah because of her wealth was also baseless. He never took any initiative in marrying her; rather, it was Khadijah who proposed to him, impressed by the integrity of his personality, his noble character and his laudable values of life.

Further, it may be observed that the Prophet had hardly any choice in his marriages, as God planned most of his marriages. Even in the case of his marriage with Khadijah, it was the will of God that was revealed in Surah Ad-Dhuha

Did He not find you poor, and made you self-sufficient".
Ad-Dhuha: 93:8

Considering the difficult task ahead, that required financial support, God had chosen a wealthy woman for him. Khadijah's wealth was utilized for the noble cause of spreading the new faith.

It will be interesting to note that in the fifth or sixth year of Prophethood, his opponents tried to stop him from preaching Islam.When all efforts failed, they tempted him with wealth and beauty. They offered him the most beautiful woman of Arabia. Had he any sexual desire, as pointed by his opponents, he would have accepted their offer, as he had only one wife at that time and she was fifty year old.

It is also important to note that during this period his opponents had severely criticized him and condmned his behavior. They went to the extent of calling him a mad man, but none of them ever passed a remark against his character.

In the second phase of his life, between the ages of fifty-one to sixty-three, no doubt he married ten women, but each marriage had a purpose behind it. After the death of Khadijah, he married Sawda, a widow of his own age. Had he been led by sexual appetite, as alleged by his critics, he could have easily married a young girl. Although he married Aisha at the same time, she came to live with him after three years, and for those three years, Sawda was his only wife.

He married Aisha, the daughter of his close friend Abu Bakr, and Hafsah, the daughter of Umar bin Khattab, mainly to strengthen the bonds of friendship and also to pay them back for their selfless services, as, to be the wife of the Prophet was the greatest honor for any woman. The women, by marrying him, automatically became the Mothers of Believers.

The answer to the question why the Prophet had so many wives in such a short span of time needs to be divided into two parts.

First, it requires a detailed study of the political situation prevailing in Madina and around. Even though the Prophet had laid the foundation of an Islamic State, and there was great enthusiasm over it among Muslims, he had to confront severe opposition from different quarters. The Quraish were waiting for an opportunity to destroy the rising tide of Islam. Moreover, there were many Jewish tribes that were giving a continuous headache to the Prophet.

There was a gap of less than two years between the battles of Uhud and Al-Ahazab, and during this period, the Prophet and his followers did not have rest even for a day. Although Muslims were victorious in many battles, the Prophet realized that war was not the only solution to expand the boundaries of Islam. As God entrusted him with the important task of spreading His message, the Prophet was keen to exploit all the avenues available to him. One of the ways to overcome animosity was the instrument of marriage. In Arabia, great importance was attached to matrimonial alliance. A son-in-law enjoyed great respect. Marriage used to end all enmity and ill will between two parties. Prophet Muhammad(S), an intelligent statesman, took advantage of this and accepted girls of different communities and tribes as his wives, creating permanent bonds of friendship. His eleven wives belonged to eleven different tribes and communities. The impact of his wives on spreading Islam was far reaching.

Umm Salamah was the daughter of the family to which Abu Jahal and Khalid bin Waleed belonged. Umm Habiba was the daughter of Abu Sufyan. Both Abu Jahal and Abu Sufyan were once bitter enemies of the Prophet, but these marriages to a great extent served to patch up the differences. Abu Sufyan never opposed the Prophet after that marriage. Safiyah was from the Jewish tribe while Juwayriah was from Banu Mustalaq tribe.When the Prophet married them, the fire of enmity between these communities cooled down.[4]

One of the important reasons of the several marriages was the education and training of women. The Prophet realized the significance of education for the women as a means of uplifting the community as a whole.It is evident from history that not only during the lifetime of the Prophet but even decades after his death, his wives continued to disseminate the teachings of Islam. This of course would not have been possible if he had only one or two wives.

Another argument with regard to the numerous marriages of the

Prophet is the fact that God planned everything. In fact, the Prophet had very little choice even with regard to his personal affairs.

Surah Al-Ahzab gives details about the Prophet's wives. It says:

> ***O Prophet! We have made lawful to you the wives to whom you have given their dowers; and those ladies whom your right hand possess (from the prisoners of war) whom Allah has assigned to you, and the daughters of your paternal uncles and aunts, and the daughters of maternal uncles and aunts, who have migrated with you, and the believing woman, who gave herself to the Prophet. If the Prophet desires to marry her - this permission is exclusively for you and not for the other believers. We have granted you this privilege as an exception, so that no blame may be attached to you. Allah is Forgiving and Merciful. It should be unlawful to you O Muhammad to marry more women after this. Al-Ahzab:33:50-52.***

From the facts mentioned above it becomes clear that the multiple marriages of the Prophet were not by choice, but were planned by God so that His message reached different segments of society.

Marriage with Aisha

Some critics have also pointed to his marriage to Aisha, who was only six or seven years old at the time of the marriage. When she came to live with the Prophet, she was nine or ten years old. [5] However, this marriage did not raise any criticism or ill feelings among the Quraish, the reason being that in those days, marriages of young girls constituted a common feature of the Arab society. The Prophet's two daughters, Ruqayya and Umm Kulthum were married to his Uncle Abu Lahab's sons before Prophethood. As the girls did not reach the age of puberty, they were living with their father and the marriages were not consummated. Abdul Muttalib married a young girl at the age of seventy. Abu Bakr and Umar both had asked for the hand of Fatima, the youngest daughter of the Prophet, even though both of them were having wives and were much older than her.[6] Umar married the daughter of Ali and Fatima when he was Amir-ul-Momineen, although Umm Kulthum was just a young child. [7]

In contrast to this, there were many examples of men marrying women who were much older than them. The best example was the Prophet himself, who married Khadijah who was fifteen years older than him. Zayd married Umm Ayman, who was at least twenty years older than him. These examples show that in matrimonial alliances, other considerations were dominant factors rather than the age. Hence, this question has to be looked at in the right context and not from today's point of view.

There was another strong reason for Aisha's marriage to the Prophet. The Prophet saw Aisha twice in his dream. An angel brought Aisha, wrapped in a silken cloth, and told him that this was his wife. [8] However, the Prophet did not reveal this to anybody before his marriage.

Marriage With Zaynab bint Jahsh

It was this marriage that attrached criticism. It also created suspicion in the minds of some of the believers. To have a clear understanding of the situation, one needs to look into the politico-social background and the Quranic verses.

Although the Prophet had laid down the foundation of an Islamic State in Madina, he did not have peace of mind, as enemies were bent on the destruction of the new state. As soon as the marriage took place, there arose a storm of propaganda against the Prophet. The polytheists, the hypocrites and the Jews were filled with jealousy at the Prophet's triumphs in battlefields that followed one after the other. As they could not succeed through warfare, they tried to tarnish his character. They resorted to the lowest means possible of fabricating false stories.

His marriage with Zaynab gave good ground for criticism, as she was the fifth wife of the Prophet, whereas God had permitted not more than four living wives to Muslims. Moreover, she was the divorced wife of his adopted son, who was like a daughter-in-law to him. In the Arab community, the adopted son was treated like a real son. It was but natural that this marriage should give rise to a wave of criticism.

The Prophet's enemies fabricated a wrong story that the Prophet fell in love with Zaynab when he once went to her house and she was not properly dressed. This allegation is baseless. Zaynab was his first cousin, they were constantly in contact with each other and it was not the first time that the Prophet had seen her. If the Prophet had any such feeling he would have married her in her youth and not when she had crossed thirty. [9] Again, it was the Prophet who had arranged her marriage to Zayd.

Various verses in the surah Al-Ahzab clearly explain why the Prophet had to enter into this marriage. To have a proper understanding of the situation, one should also look into the customs and traditions of the Arab community of that period. In pre-Islamic days or what is called the period of Jahliyyah (ignorance), there were many deep-rooted undesirable practices, one of which involved the practice of adoption. The adopted son was not only treated as a biological son, but had all the privileges of a legal son. He had the right of inheritance and his marriage with the daughters of his foster mother was prohibited. The practice had also given rise to many abuses, depriving the legal inheritors of their shares. These were also against the legal provisions laid down in the Quran regarding marriage, divorce, inheritance and other family issues. To put an end to this ancient practice, promulgation of laws was not sufficient. Th is needed strong practical demonstration that the Prophet, who was a model for thousands of his followers, could have given.

Surah Al-Ahzab clearly indicates that

> *O Prophet, remember when you said to the one whom Allah, as well as, you had favoured;"keep your wife in wedlock and fear Allah" you sought to hide in your heart what Allah intended to reveal; you were afraid of the people whereas it would have been more appropriate to fear Allah. So when Zayd fulfilled his desire, we gave her to you in marriage, so that there remains no hindrance for the believers to wed the wives of their adopted sons, if they divorced them. And Allah's command had to be carried out. There can be no blame attached to the Prophet for doing what is sanctioned to him by Allah ... Muhammad is not the father of any of your men, but is the Rasool of Allah and the seal of the Prophets. Allah has the knowledge of all things.*
> *Al-Ahzab: 33:37-40*

The Prophet was hesitant to marry Zaynab, for he had expected criticism, though he had an indication that God wanted him to marry her so as to set a precident. God knew what was in the heart of the Prophet and warned him that he should fear Allah and not the people. Some of his critics had given a twist to the words "you sought to hide in your heart". They interpreted this to mean his desire for Zaynab, though the Surah further makes the meaning of this sentence very clear when it says "we give her to you in marriage, so that there remains no hindrance for the believers to wed the wives of their adopted sons, if they divorced them".

God himself arranged this marriage and gave no time to the Prophet to decide. In spite of such a clear explanation, the critics gave it a twist and indulged in character assassination.

Mothers Of Believers

While God has given an edge to man over woman in some respects, He has given a special position to woman, which is exclusively her domain. According to a saying of the Prophet, Heaven lies under the feet of the mother. Motherhood is a special honor, accompanied by great responsibilities. A mother is the symbol of love, affection and sacrifice. She sacrifices her time, energy, comfort and money for the sake of her children.

Not only does she give birth to a child, but through her training and education enables a child to find a proper place in society. Her influence on the young mind leaves an ever-lasting impression. However, in societies where women simply give birth but have no time to spare for the children, the children go astray, indulge in undesirable activities and damage the social structure. Many problems of today's advanced societies are due to the fact that women, in their zeal for the equality of sexes, ignore their primary role as mothers. Some women try to make up for the loss, while at the same time competing with men for equality and bringing heavy pressure on themselves and the household. If only women could balance their primary responsibility of proper upbringing of their children against their push for equality in society half of the ills of modern society could perhaps be eliminated.

In the Quran, God has addressed the wives of the Prophet as Mothers of Believers, an honor that does not find a parallel in history.

> *The Prophet is closer to the believers than their*
> *own selves and his wives are their mothers*
> *Al-Ahzab: 33:6*

The Quran says that they enjoy a special status. In today's context, special status means special privileges enjoyed by a person. In the context of the Quran, this great honor was accompanied by certain restrictions.

God warned them:

O wives of the Prophet you are not like other women.
Al-Ahzab: 33:32

O wives of the Prophet! If any of you commit an open indecency, her
punishment will be increased to double and this is easy for Allah.
Al-Ahzab: 33:30

The reason for this strict code of conduct for them was the fact that they had to set an example for the entire society. They were not like other women who could commit mistakes and get away with them. Everyone watched the actions of these ladies and therefore they had to be very cautious at every step. Whenever any one of them took a wrong step, Allah warned them, though not by name. The idea was that the Prophet's wives had to be perfect women, judged from the point of view of behavior or character, as they played role models for thousands of women.

The Quran further explains why these restrictions were provided for them. It says:

......O women of the household of Rasool, Allah only intends to
remove un-cleanliness from you and to purify you completely
Al-Ahzab: 33:33

Although they had the distinction of being the wives of the Messenger of Allah, they enjoyed hardly any luxury of life. The Prophet never liked that his wives or children and grandchildren wear expensive clothes or jewelery. Many a time, they did not have even basic amenities like proper food or clothing and they had to starve for days together. Aisha had mentioned that once they did not have anything to cook for three consecutive days. They survived on black dates. Most of the time, they could not even light a lamp at night for want of oil. The life of the wives of the Prophet was stark in contrast to the wives of the kings and emperors who lived in luxury.

Apart from these restrictions, God had also given them many responsibilities. The Quran describes the role, when it says:

Establish Salah, pay Zakat, and obey Allah and his Rasool.
Al-Ahzab: 33: 33

Remember the Revelation of Allah and wise
sayings which are recited in your houses.
Al-Ahzab: 33:34

These few lines place heavy responsibilities on the Prophet's wives. Praying regularly and paying Zakat were obligatory for them. They also had to remember the Revelations of Allah, which means the Quran, and the sayings of the Prophet. They were expected to disseminate these to other people as the Prophet's Sunnah (traditions) that formed an important part of Muslim laws then and subsequently. The wives had the responsibility of remembering them in the proper context. Traditions have been greatly enriched by the contribution of these wives. Aisha had contributed 2210 traditions, Umm Salamah 378, Maymunah 76, Umm Habiba 65, Hafsah 60 and the traditions of other wives put together were 33.[10] Hafsah was good at reading and writing. She played a remarkable role at the time of the compilation of the Quran.

Traditions From The Wives Of The Prophet

S.No.	Name of the Wife	No. of Traditions
1.	Aisha	2210
2	Umm Salamah	378
3	Maymunah	76
4.	Umm Habiba	65
5.	Hafsah	60
6.	Safiyah	10
7.	Sawda	5
	Total Traditions	2804

Source: Ali Asghar Choudhari: Ummat Ki Mayen, 1994, p. 14.

As Allah had instructed the wives to recite the Quran, all of them spent a lot of time in reciting the Quran. Three of them - Aisha, Hafsah and Umm Salamah - were *Hafizatul* Quran.[11] During the life of the Prophet, and especially after his death, there used to be women's gatherings in their houses, where they used to teach the Quran and discuss various issues pertaining to day-to-day life, in the light of the Quran. Dissemination of Quranic knowledge was one of the reasons for the Prophet's multiple marriages. They did contribute substantially in the success of his mission. Many of his wives had a long period of widowhood. Umm Salamah was the last to die. She lived for 48 years as a widow. Aisha was a widow for 44 years. During these long periods their contribution to Islamic history, culture and civilization was immense It may be noted that although Islam encourages marriage of widows, in the case of the wives of the Prophet, there were strict instructions regarding the remarriage of the Prophet's wives after his death.

It is not proper for you to annoy the Rasool of Allah,
nor ever to marry his wives after him: this would
be a grievous offence in the sight of Allah.
Al-Ahzab: 33:53

The reason for this restriction is obvious. Once they have been declared as Mothers, all Muslims become their sons and idiomatically no son could marry his Mother.

Allah had also instructed them to pay Zakat, so that they may establish a good example for others. Most of the wives were so generous that they used to distribute all their money to the poor and the needy; their pecuniary status was unenviable. It is narrated that once Abdullah bin Zubair sent Aisha 1000 dirhams. Aisha asked her servant to distribute the entire money among the poor. That day she was fasting. She did not keep a single dirham for herself. When the servant reminded her, she said that she should have told her earlier

In Mecca and in the early period in Madina, the Prophet's wives did not observe Hijab even though Umar had requested the Prophet that he should ask his wives to observe Hijab.[13] However, the Prophet was waiting for God's order. When Allah gave His orders:

O Prophet! Enjoin your wives, daughters and the Believing women,
that they should draw their outer garment over their persons. That
is more proper, so that they may be recognized and not bothered.
Al-Ahzab: 33:59

Curtains were hung not only over the doors of the Prophet's house, but also in the house of every Muslim because the Prophet's house was a model for everyone.[14]

Although after this Ayah the Prophet's wives used to cover their faces, this did not come in the way of their performing normal duties. They used to go to the mosque and pray.[15] They accompanied the Prophet to the battlefields. Aisha and Umm Salamah served the wounded soldiers on the battlefields. After the Prophet passed away, Aisha even went to the battlefield and addressed the soldiers.[16]

This brief survey of the Mothers of Believers shows that although it was a great honor to be the wife of the Prophet, it was not always easy to act in the manner prescribed by God. In spite of the fact that they were the best women, chosen by God, they did commit some mistakes, for which they had to repent.

The Prophet As A Husband

The Prophet's role as a husband may be divided into two phases. The first phase was from the time of his marriage with Khadijah untill her death and the second phase was after her death till the Prophet's demise. The first phase was of twenty-five years, while the second one was of only thirteen years.

The First Phase

The first phase of his married life was perhaps his happiest period. He had no financial worries. He had a happy family, consisting of his wife and four daughters. His two daughters Zaynab and Ruqayya were already married. After Prophethood, he had a very tough period since he had to face humiliation and frustration all the time. Three years of social boycott by the Quraish was a period of great suffering for the whole family. In spite of all these tensions, there was the consolation that there was some one at home who understood him, believed him, loved him, and was concerned about him which was a great comfort to the Prophet. But for Khadijah, things would have been different for the Prophet. There was never any misunderstanding or tension between the couple. They had a very happy and satisfied married life. The Prophet was deeply in love with her. This was evident from the fact that he used to praise her even after her death, in front of his other wives.

The Second Phase

The second phase was of thirteen years, when the Prophet married ten wives. One died within a few months.[17] The other nine survived till his death. Although it was a difficult period, he played his role of husband in a most befitting manner. It was not easy to maintain harmonious relations among so many wives, but he always tried to do full justice. He tried to give equal treatment to all, but at the same time he realized that he had no control as far as love was concerned. It was an open secret that Aisha was his beloved wife. He himself realized this weakness and prayed to God, "If I have unintentionally shown more love to one of them than the others and this would have been injustice, so O Lord I take refuge in your grace for these things which are beyond my power".

The Prophet had strictly divided his time, among his wives. He used to go to each one of them by turn. It was his routine to go to each wife in the evening after *Asar* prayer, spending some time with her and then used to stay in the apartment of one who had her turn. All the other wives also used to come there for chat. The time was also utilized for discussion and decisions. The atmosphere used to be generally very cordial. He never tried to favor one over the other.

Although he had occupied such a high position as the Messenger of Allah and the founder of the Islamic State, at home he was altogether a different person. He never boasted of his position. He never caused tension in his house due to his outside worries or problems. He always used to enter the house with a smiling face, unlike many husbands of the present time, who expect great respect and complete silence at home. In many houses, even children are scared of their fathers and there is a communication gap between them. With the Prophet, things were different.

Today, if a wife is not working, the husband does not like to share the household work. The entire burden has to be borne by the wife. Although the Prophet was always busy and had so many things to look after, still he used to share the household work. Aisha has narrated that, "He was like one of you at home, yet he was the most lenient and most considerate. His spirits were high at all times, smiling and even joining in laughter at times. He was ready to give a helping hand to his wives in the ordinary work of the house, sew his own clothes and mended his shoes. However, when the call for prayer was made, he dropped everything and hurried to the mosque".[18]

The Prophet used to tell the people "do not make your home a graveyard" and "he is the best person who is good to his household." Today we find that there is a big difference between what people preach and what they practice at home. Most men are very polite, patient and understanding at their work place and with their friends, but the moment they enter their houses, they change colors and start bossing over their wives and children. There was no contradiction between the Prophet's words and his actions.

The Prophet was very particular to give dower (Mehar) to his wives. Even today, payment of dower is essential. However, instead of giving it in the beginning, it is generally given either at a later date or at the time of divorce. Many a time, women are asked to forsake it as an act of mercy. The usual dower for the Prophet's wives was between 400 to 500 dirhams. Today, many people insist on a very high dower as a means of security for their girls, which is not the right concept.

In Islam, it is obligatory for the bridegroom to pay dower to his bride. There is no burden on the bride's side to pay anything. Dower actually is a symbolic payment that indicates that the bridegroom will bear all the financial responsibilities of the family in future. Today, in some communities, the word dower has given birth to dowry, which includes cash, gold, and other items given to the bride and groom by the bride's family. In many cases, instead of being a voluntary act, it has become an obligatory one. When demands are not fulfilled, it leads to serious situations to the extent of annulment of marriages. The Muslim community needs to focus attention on the correct meaning and sprit of dower so as to ensure the happiness of married life.

The Prophet had allotted an apartment separately to each wife and that was her property. Some of these were purchased afterwards for the expansion of the Mosque. It is interesting to note that many of his wives had come from well to do families. They were used to a very comfortable life style, but in the company of the Prophet, who himself lived a simple life, they also got used to the same modest way of life. In those days the basic needs of the people were very limited. The wives just had what was essential for survival. The great thing the Prophet taught his wives was patience which is a great virtue, but difficult to acquire.

The wives did not have much household work to do. Neither were their houses big nor did they have much furniture, [19] even cooking was minimum. Many a time, there was nothing to cook for days together. Moreover, they did not have children, with the result that they had a lot of leisure time. Their time was mostly utilized in prayers and recitation of the Quran.

There used to be women's gatherings in the house. The idea was the expansion of knowledge and training for their future task. It was realized that unless women were properly educated and get rid of orthodox practices, no change and advancement in society was possible. The Prophet had the challenging task of molding the future of the society. He was very particular that his wives should be instrumental in enlightening other women.

There was always competition among the wives for the favor of God and His Messenger. The Prophet used to do *Itikaf* (seclusion to concentrate on prayer to Allah) in the month of Ramadan, normally in the last ten days. Aisha has narrated that once the Prophet intended to practice *Itikaf* and when he reached the place to perform *Itikaf*, he saw the tents of Aisha, Hafsah, and Zaynab. So he said "do you consider that they intended to do Al-Birr (righteousness) by doing this? And he did not perform *Itikaf* in Ramadan but did it in the month of Shawwal.[20]

He always made it a point to take at least one of his wives with him when he used to go out, even on the battlefield. Lots decided which wife would accompany him. All his wives accompanied him when he went to perform Haj. All his wives were by his side at the time of his death, even though he was in Aisha's apartment.

Inspite of the great efforts of the Prophet to maintain a friendly and harmonious atmosphere at home, some time there was tension in the household. It was but natural, as all the wives loved the Prophet very much and everyone wanted his love and attention. Any encroachment on their rights was resisted. This was especially the case with Aisha. When Aisha came to live with the Prophet, only Swada was there and she was a middle-aged woman. The entry of Hafsah in the household also did not bring any significant change, as both Aisha and Hafsah soon became close friends. However, with the increase in the number of wives, especially Umm Salamah, who was supposedly very beautiful, and Zaynab who was not only the Prophet's cousin but her marriage was indicated by God and with the arrival of Juwayriah and Safiyah, who were young and beautiful, the envies started surfacing. On many occasions, the wives were divided into groups, one led by Aisha in which Hafsah, Swada and Safiyah were included and the other headed by Zaynab, which included all the other wives.

There were some incidents that threw light on the politics of the household .God himself had taken cognizance of them. There were at least three incidents of great significance where there were lapses on the part of the Prophet's wives and God had warned them. They pertain to:

i) A situation where the Prophet had to take a vow not to do something again

ii) The Prophet had told a secret to one of his wives but she could not confine that to herself and told the secret to another wife.

iii) The temporary separation of the Prophet from his wives.

There are three important Revelations pertaining to these incidents. In Surah Al- Tahreem, God says:

O Prophet, why do you make something unlawful, which Allah has made lawful to you in seeking to please your wives
Al- Tahreem: 66:1

In the same Surah, He further elaborates:

When the Prophet disclosed a matter in confidence to one of his consorts, and she then divulged it (to another), and Allah made it known to him, he confirmed part thereof and repudiated a part. Then when he told her thereof, she said, "Who told thee this?"He said, "He told me Who knows and is well-acquainted (with all things)."

If ye two turn in repentance to Him, your hearts are indeed so inclined; But if ye back up each other against him, truly Allah is his Protector, and Gabriel, and (every) righteous one among those who believe,- and furthermore, the angels - will back (him) up.

It may be, if he divorced you (all), that Allah will give him in exchange consorts better than you,- who submit (their wills), who believe, who are devout, who turn to Allah in repentance, who worship (in humility), who travel (for Faith) and fast,- previously married or virgins.

Al Tahreem: 6:3-5.

When the period of temporary separation from his wives was over, God revealed the following Ayah:

O Prophet say to your wives: if you desire the life of this world and it glittering then come I shall give you these and let you go in an honourable way. But if you seek Allah and his Rasool

> ***and the home hereafter, then you should rest assured that Allah
> has prepared a great reward for those of you who are good.***
> ***Al-Ahzab: 33:28,29***

The Wives' Plotting

The jealousy of the wives had gone to such an extent that they made
a plot against their own husband. The Prophet used to visit all his wives
after the *Asar* prayer. It is reported that once or twice when he went to
Zaynab bint Jahsh, he stayed there for a pretty long time. The reason was
that Zaynab had got some honey and the Prophet loved sweet things. But
this made the other wives jealous. Aisha herself reported that "Hafsah and
I plotted together that any wife whom the Prophet visits will complain to
him that she finds his breath undesirable and will ask him whether he has
eaten any *Maghafir*.[21] As he entered upon one of his wives, she asked him
that question, to which he answered "No, but I have taken some honey at
the quarter of Zaynab .[22] It is believed that Hafsah, Umm-Salamah and
Safiyah, all asked the same question and the Prophet gave the same reply
to all of them. When Aisha asked the same question, he vowed never to
touch that again.[23]

The important point before us is that God disapproved of the behavior
of some of his wives and gave a serious warning to them. The secret was
not disclosed either by God or by the Prophet and hence it is not for us to
probe further and try to ascertain the secret. However, it only indicates
that it is not good to disclose the secrets of the family.

There are a number of things that take place between husband and wife
and if other people come to know, they may take undue advantage of the
situation and spoil their relationsship. In the case of the Prophet, this had
far reaching implications, as there were many things that were discussed
in the house. If enemies would have come to know, they could have taken
undue advantage of the situation. Even for all of us, it is inappropriate to
disclose the secrets of any other person.

Ila-The Prophet's Temporary Separation from His Wives

The Prophet had taken a vow not to see his wives for a month. He
retired to the upper portion of the house that was generally used as an area
for storage. There was not even a proper mattress for him. When Umar saw
the Prophet in such a condition he started weeping. The Prophet's decision

created great uneasiness among his companions and believers. Most of them were under the wrong impression that the Prophet had divorced his wives and they were worried and disturbed. But when Umar ascertained the facts, there was a wave of happiness everywhere.

At the end of his period of separation, God revealed the Surah Tahreem, which gave the option to his wives either to get divorced from the Prophet for the sake of the glitters of this world or to be with him and God assured them of a good reward. After the revelation, the Prophet went to his wives, starting with Aisha and told her not to take a hasty decision but to consult her parents. After hearing that, Aisha replied, "Is there any need to consult my parents? Indeed, I desire Allah and his Messenger and the abode of the next world". After this he went to the other wives, and they also gave the same answer as given by Aisha.

There are many things that need clarification. What was the reason for the Prophet to take such a drastic step? Most of the time he was very patient and tolerant of his wives' behavior. Also, what was the date of this incident? Opinion is divided on both the questions. Some believe that it was mainly on the issue of enhancement of allowances of his wives. They reported that once when Abu Bakr and Umar went to see the Prophet, they found the Prophet surrounded by his wives, who were talking very loudly. When they asked the Prophet, he said, "They were asking for what I don't have". On hearing that, Abu Bakr and Umar both scolded their daughters.

The argument that the Prophet had taken such a strong action merely on the demand of enhancement of allowances of his wives does not sound very convincing. Most likely, he must have been mentally disturbed by the continuous tension created by his wives, mainly due to their mutual jealousies.

There are two important issues with regard to these incidents. One is the date of occurrence and the other whether they were isolated incidents or part of a planned scheme.

Opinion is again divided on both the issues. Maudoodi claims that the incident of enhancement of allowance took place in 5th AH when the Prophet had only four wives (Sawda, Aisha, Hafsah, and Umm-Salamah).[25] Muhammad Farooqu-Azam Malik is also of the view that Surah Al-Ahzab was revealed in in 5th AH [26]. Shibli Nawmani says it was revealed in early 9th AH.[27]

There is also difference of opinion with regard to the second question. Some writers are of the view that they were not isolated issues, but part of a long pre planned conspiracy, in which non-believers had a share. As the enemies of Islam could not defeat the Muslims, they started sowing seeds of discontent among the wives to destroy the house of the Prophet.

In Sahih al Bukhari's chapter on Marriage Contract, there is a report on the authority of Abbas, clarifying that the alliance of the wives, the Prophet's isolation, the disclosure of the secret and the revelation offering the choice, are all part of a single event.[28] The truth needs to be ascertained with authenticity, but the fact is that the discontent and jealousy among the wives had reached a climax. The presence of Maria, the slave girl, and the birth of his son Ibrahim had added fuel to the fire.

One needs to understand the psychology of wives. If a wife is not able to give birth to a child, she feels frustrated and faces a psychological problem. While in the case of the Prophet's wives, out of eleven, he had children only from his first wife Khadijah. Although later on, he had nine living wives and some of them were very young but none of them had bore any child. It is but natural that when the Prophet had a son from Maria it gave rise to a hysterical atmosphere.

To conclude, in spite of the Prophet's efforts there was sometimes tension in the house. As long as he had only one wife, there was no family tension; hence it is always desirable not to have more than one wife at a time. Polygamy is permitted but should not be taken as a matter of right. Muslims generally have a wrong notion about this.

If we closely examine the personal life of the Prophet, solutions for many problems of married life can be found. The patience with which he handled all problems, the lively atmosphere at home and the sharing of household work not only gave a sense of participation but also a feeling of equality and concern for each other. In present day society, there is a lack of tolerance between the husband and the wife. This has resulted in a large number of divorces and broken homes, creating psychological and emotional problems for their children. We need to learn the secrets of maintaining harmonious relations between the husband and the wife from the life of the Prophet.

References And Notes

1. All the writers have generally agreed on the existence of eleven wives. The difference of opinion arises mainly with regard to the status of Maria and Rehana, the two slave girls.
2. Muhammad Razi ul Islam Nadwi: Rasool Kareem ki Isdowaji Zindagi; Tahqeeqet-e-Islam (Quarterly) April-June 2000 Aligarh India
3. Maudoodi Moulana Sayed Abu Ala: Talkhees ul Quran. Markazi Maktabah Islami, Delhi 1984, p. 138
4. Ibid, p. 666
5. Bukhari, Muslim, Sulaman Nadvi, Afrog Hassan, Martin Lings, Mubarakpuri, and Abbass Madani, all have agreed that Aisha was 6 or 7 years old at the time of marriage and 9 or 10 when she joined the Prophet in Madina. Of late some writers have contradicted this view and claim that she was 16 or 17 year old at the time of marriage. I do not wish to enter into controversy. I personally feel that the first version is correct, as there are a number of authentic traditions. Secondly, it is an established fact that marriage at an early age was common in Arabia at that time
6. Martin Lings, op. cit., p. 63.
7. Zakaria Bashier: Sunshine at Madina, op. cit., p. 172.
8. Bukhari and others. Also Martin Lings, op. cit.,
9. Ali Asghar, Chowdhari: Ummat Ke Mayeen, Islamic Publications, Lahore, Pakistan, 1994, p. 236.
10. Ibid., p. 14.
11. Zakaria Bashier, Sunshine at Madina, op. cit. p. 47.
12. Umm Salamah was 36 year old at the time of the Prophet's death. She died at the age of 84. Aisha was 18 or 19 year old when she became a widow. She died at the age of 63.
13. Maudoodi: Talkheesul Quran, op. cit., p. 972.
14. Ibid.
15. Martin Lings, op. cit., p. 237
16. Asghar Ali, op. cit. p. 126.
17. Zaynab bint Kuzaymah.

18. Ibn Sa'd: Tabaqat. Vol. I, p. 364 quoted by Zakaria Bashier. Sunshine at Madina op. cit. p. 154.

19. The apartment was a room of 15 feet by 9 feet with a very low ceiling.

20. The Translation of the Meaning of Summarized Sahih Al Baukhari. Dr. Mohd Mohsin Khan, Maktba, Darus-Saalm, Riyad, 1994, pp. 461, 462.

21. A flower with some undesirable smell.

22. Haykal, Muhammad Husayan: The Life of Muhammad: Translation by Ismail Ragi , 1976, p. 435.

23. Ibid.

24. Ibid. p. 436. a) Martin Lings is also of the same view op. cit. p. 277. b) Shibli Nawmani is of a different view. In his commentary on Bukari, he says "As to the occasion when this verse was revealed, the true report is that it refers to the honey affairs and not any affair about Maria, which is described in books other than two authentic collections (Bukhari and Muslims) Siratul- Nabi, Vol. IIp. 211.

25. Maudoodi, Talkhees -ul-Quran, op. cit., p. 661.

26. Malik, Muhammad Farooqui-i-Azam: Al-Quran. The Institute of Islamic knowledge Houston, U.S.A., p. 549.

27. Shibli Nawmani, op. cit., Vol. II, p. 201.

28. Ibid, p. 208.

Part III

Live Sketches Of The Wives Of The Prophet

	Names	Age at the time of marriage	Prophet's age at the time of marriage.	Marital status	Age at the time of death	Companionship with the Prophet	Period of widowhood
1	Khadi-jah bint Khuwailid	40	25	Widow Twice married	65	25	Nil
2	Sawda Bint Zama	50	51	Widow	72	12	10
3	Aisha bint Abu Bakr	6 or 7 9 or 10	51,53	Never married	63	10	44
4	Hafsa Bint Umar Khattab	20	54	Widow	59	9	30
5	Zaynab Bint Khuzaymah	30	55	Widow Married thrice	30	Few months	Nil
6	Umm Sala-mah bint Omaiya	29	56	Widow	84	7	48
7	Zaynab Bint Jah'sh	34	57	Divorced	53	6	13
8	Juwayriah Bint Harith	20	57	Widow	65	6	39
9	Umm -Hbiba	36	57	Widow	72	6	30
10	Safiyah Bint Huyayy	17	57	Widow Thrice married	60	6	37
11	Maymuna Bint Harris	N.A.	59	Widow Thrice married	80	4	N. A.

Khadijah Bint Khuwailid

1.	Parents name	Father: Khuwailid Bin Asad Mother: Fatima Bin Zaidi
2.	Age at the time of marriage	40 years
3.	Prophet's age at the time of marriage	25 years
4.	Marital status	Widow – twice married earlier
5.	Children with the previous husbands	2 sons and 1 daughter
6.	Children with the prophet	2 sons and 4 daughters
7.	Age at the time of death	65 years
8.	Companionship with the Prophet	25 years
9.	Buried at	Mecca – Hajon mountain

Khadijah belonged to a noble family of the Quraish. Her father was Khldwaylid bin Asad. Her mother was Fatima Bin Zaidi. She was known as Khadijahtul Kubra because of her noble nature. She was twice married before she married Muhammad. Her first husband was Abu Hala. She had two sons from him, Hala and Haris. After her husband's death she was married to Ateeq bin Abid. She had one daughter by name Hina, from him.

After his death, she preferred to remain widow until she met Muhammad. Khadijah was a most respected and a very rich lady. Perhaps no person in Mecca had more wealth than her. She had extensive trade and was able to manage it very well. She was very graceful and charming, in spite of the fact that she was not young. All eligible men wanted to marry her, but none of them came close to her expectations. She was looking for someone who had a very high character and one who was not looking to marry her just for the sake of her wealth. Since she could not find anyone of her choice, she preferred to remain unmarried.

Khadijah used to send her merchandise to other places by hiring people on commission. When Muhammad was about 25 years old, she heard about his honesty, integrity and truthfulness, and offered him double the commission. Muhammad went to Syria to trade her merchandise.

Khadijah's servant Maysarah accompanied him. Muhammad made good profit, and on his return, he bought merchandise and sold it doubling the profit. When he came back to Mecca, Maysarah gave a detailed account of his trade mission. He had high regards not only for Muhammad's honesty and integrity but also for the treatment he had meted out to him. He never treated him as a servant but as his equal. Maysarah also narrated what a Monk had told about Muhammad, "None other than a Prophet is sitting beneath that tree".[1]

Khadijah was greatly impressed by the description of Maysarah. She had also met Muhammad many a time in connection with her business and found him to be a very noble person. She considered him to be the right person for life partner, but she was not sure of his response, as she was much older than him. She asked her friend Nafisah to talk to him. When Nafisah asked him why he did not marry, he replied that he did not have the means to marry. When Nafisah said, "If thou were given the means and if thou were bidden to an alliance where there is beauty and property, nobility and abundance, wouldst thou not consent?" Muhammad asked, "Who is she?" "Khadijah" said Nafisah. "And how could such a marriage be mine?" asked Muhammad. "Leave that to me" said Nafisah. "For my part I am willing," replied Muhammad.[2]

Khadijah called Muhammad and she told him that she was interested in marrying him. A meeting of the elders followed this. It is reported that Abu Talib gave twenty she camels on his behalf as dower. There is another tradition that he gave 500 gold dirhams in marriage. [3] After the marriage, a dinner was given which according to the standard of that time was a very good one. Khadijah's friends played the Daf. [4] As Muhammad did not have a house of his own, he came to live in Khadijah's house. It is believed that she had a big mansion, with many servants.

Muhammad and Khadijah lived together for 25 years. The idea of a second marriage never entered his mind, although it was common in Arabia. Their married life was a very happy and peaceful. There was no friction and no difference of opinion.

It is difficult to find another example in history where a wife had been so devoted and had done so much for her husband. When she married Muhammad, she was the richest woman in Mecca, but in the subsequent 25 years she spent everything for the sake of her husband. She provided him not only physical and financial comforts but more important was her moral support. She was a very good friend, sometimes a philosopher and guide. She had great faith in her husband. She knew he had never told a lie in his life. She had a very high opinion of her husband and that was the reason that when the whole world looked down at him and did not believe him, it was she who gave him confidence. Sometimes, he himself did not know what to do. When he received the First Revelation, he came home trembling and shivering as a result of that unusual occurrence, he was not sure whether it was a dream or a reality. But when Khadijah listened to him, she did not have any doubt. She realized that something extraordinary had happened to her husband. "Do not worry, for by Him who has dominion over Khadijah's soul, I hope that you are the Prophet of this nation. Allah will never humiliate you, you are true to your words, you help those who are in need, you support the weak, you feed the guests and you respond to the call of those who are in distress". In order to get further assurance, Khadijah took him to her cousin Waraqah, who was a learned man of his time and was considered a master of the Torah and the Gospel. Waraqah immediately recognized him as the same person whose arrival was predicted in the Holy Scriptures. Khadijah's happiness knew no bounds. She said to her husband, "Blessed be thou, chosen one! There is no God but Allah and thou art His chosen one".

Many a time after prophethood, Muhammad would return home sad and disheartened, but she would always be ready with encouragement and support. She did her best to comfort him and he would soon regain his cheerful, optimistic attitude. For this unwavering support, Gabriel once came to the Prophet and told him to carry Allah's greetings to Khadijah and gave her the happy news that she had a special home in heaven where she would enjoy total bliss and happiness.[5] According to Bukhari, once Gabriel informed the Prophet that Khadijah was bringing something in a pot, and he should convey Allah's and his own compliments to her.

Khadijah had the honor to be the first person to accept Islam. She was also the first to perform prayers with the Prophet, after Gabriel taught the Prophet how to perform prayer. Khadijah's influence in spreading the new faith was immense. Not only his immediate household accepted the faith, but also she could influence many women to embrace Islam. In the first three-year period, there were 133 persons who accepted Islam, in which there were 27 women.[6]

Khadijah's role in strengthening the path of Islam was great. She was a silent worker. The amount of support, both financial and moral, she had given to the new faith was immeasurable. The richest lady had spent all her wealth in supporting the new faith. Whatever little money was left, she used it at the time of social boycott for purchasing the essentials of life.

The hardship of that three-year period had adversely affected her health. Khadijah was not used to hardship. Before her marriage to the Prophet, she had a very luxurious life. She never had any financial worries and there were many servants to look after her. Gradually, things changed. In the last few years before her death and especially during the social boycott, the whole family had to undergo serious social and financial stress. She had become very weak .After the ban was over she could not survive and died at the age of 65 years. There is a difference of opinion about the exact date of her death. Some sources indicate that Abu Talib died a few months after her, while others claim that she followed Abu Talib.

The first ten years of her married life were comparatively peaceful, but a few years prior to Prophehood, the Prophet was disturbed with things around him. He used to retire to a cave, known as Hira, and used to stay there for days together, especially in Ramadan. She never objected to his staying there. She was a perfect companion, a woman of extraordinary wisdom and intelligence, an exceptional person of grace and dignity. She had a deep insight into human psychology. She had seen the ups and downs of life and was now able to face any difficult situation without becoming panicky.

The Prophet was deeply in love with her and always remembered her for her love and kindness. Although he married several wives after her death, which were younger than her, and very beautiful, but in his own words nobody could take the place of Khadijah. Aisha was very jealous of her. Once Aisha asked him "Why do you keep thinking of that old woman who is dead so long when Allah has given you such fine wives?" The Prophet replied "No, I did not get a better wife than her…she believed in me when none else did. She embraced Islam when people disbelieved me and she helped and comforted me with her personal wealth when there was none else to lend me a helping hand. I had children from her only". [7]

The Prophet had great regard for her friends, even after her death. Whenever he slaughtered an animal, he made it a point to send the meat to her friends. Once when Khadijah's sister Hala came to see the Prophet, Aisha was with him. Hala asked for permission to come inside. On hearing her voice, he was so excited and said it must be Hala, her voice being similar to Khadijah's voice.

Khadijah was an extremely generous lady. She always helped the poor and the needy. Halima, the foster mother of the Prophet used to visit them frequently. Once, when she came to see them, there was a serious drought in her place. Khadijah made her a gift of forty sheep and a howdah.

Khadijah was a very affectionate person. Along with her children, she had brought up Ali bin Abu Talib who was with them from the age of five. Although Zayd was a slave boy, the Prophet had adopted him as his son. Khadijah also brought him up.

It is believed that there is always a woman behind all great men. In the case of the Prophet, it is beyond doubt that it was Khadijah, who quietly provided physical, financial, emotional, and moral support to the Prophet. It was due to this reason that the Prophet loved her immensely and none of his wives could reach that position.

Sawda Bint Zam`a

1.	Parents name	Father: Zam`a Bin Qays Bin Shams Mother: Ash Shamush
2.	Age at the time of marriage	50 years
3.	Prophet's age at the time of marriage	51 years
4.	Marital status	Widow
5.	Children with the previous husbands	1 son
6.	Children with the prophet	None
7.	Age at the time of death	72 years
8.	Companionship with the Prophet	10 years
9.	Period of widowhood	12 years
10.	Number of traditions ascribed to her	5
11.	Buried at	Madina – Jannat ul Baqui

Sawda's father's was Zam'a bin Qays. Her mother was Ash - Shamush, from a Najjar tribe. She was married to her cousin Sakran bin Omro. After Muhammad's Prophethood, she embraced Islam along with her husband. Under her influence, many of her close relatives like Habib bin Omra, Saketh bin Omro, Malik bin Zama, Fatima bint Alaqma also embraced Islam. She belonged to the first batch of people who had migrated to Abyssinia. After her return to Abyssinia, her husband died. She was living with her old father. She had suffered a lot during her stay in Abyssinia, but her faith in Islam was very strong.

The year 619 A.D. was a year of sorrow for the Prophet. His beloved life partner, Khadijah, passed away a few months after the death of his uncle Abu Talib. The Prophet came under severe stress and strain. Both the strong pillars of his life had suddenly collapsed, leaving the Prophet rudderless, not knowing what to do. As long as Khadijah was there, she had shouldered all the household responsibilities, but now, all of a sudden the responsibility of running the household was thrust upon him. Much more difficult was the job of taking care of his young daughters, Umm Kulthum and Fatima. Outside, the house too it was a period of great tension for him.

Following the demise of Abu Talib the Quraish were now free to create as much trouble for him as possible. They left no stone unturned to humiliate him. Earlier on such occasions he used to turn to his wife, for support and comfort, but now in the house there were two young innocent girls who needed comfort and help. He was badly in need of someone who could take over the responsibilities of his household and who could give motherly affection to his daughters. Due to his household problems, he was finding it difficult to concentrate on his mission.

It was in this background that Khawla bint Hakeem, wife of Usman bin Maz'oom, who was close to the Prophet and who was taking care of his daily needs after Khadijah's death, suggested to the Prophet that he should marry again. When the Prophet asked her whom he should marry, she suggested two names. One was Sawda, who was a widow of about fifty years and another was Aisha, the six-year-old daughter of Abu Bakr.

At first sight it may look very strange about the two proposals, as there was no comparison between the two. Khawla, an intelligent lady, realized that the Prophet needed an elderly lady who could understand his problems, shoulder the responsibilities and give him peace of mind. It was difficult to expect a young girl to have these qualities, especially to give motherly treatment to his daughters. At the same time, Khawla also realized the need for a companion who could be a source of happiness to him. Prophet Muhammad(S) agreed to both proposals.

For Sawda, it was a great honor to be the wife of the Prophet. The marriage was performed and the Prophet gave her 400 dirhams as dower. It is believed that Sawda had dreamt that the moon had fallen in her lap. When she narrated her dream to her husband Sakran, he said that he would die soon and she would be married to the Prophet. His prophecy came true.[8] she had the honor of being the only wife of the Prophet after Khadijah for three years, until Aisha came into the life of the Prophet. When the Prophet migrated to Madina, Sawda was in Mecca along with his daughters for seven months. They moved to Madina when her apartment was built next to the Mosque.

Sawda was a woman who underwent great sufferings in the cause of Islam. She was devoted to the Prophet and led a very simple and pious life. Fatima and Umm Kulthum were with her for about six years until they got married. There is not a single incident quoted by historians indicating a step motherly treatment. Her apartment was adjacent to Aisha's apartment. As Aisha was even younger than Fatima, Sawda used to love her and look after her needs. Subsequently, when the Prophet divided his time equally among all other wives, Sawda, realizing her advanced age and the great affection that the Prophet had for Aisha, voluntarily gave her turn to Aisha.

Sawda was a very pious lady. She was very particular about her prayers and would spend a lot of time in prayers. Aisha remarked about Sawda, "It is Sawda, on seeing whom I wish my soul lived in her body." She was also very obedient. On the eve of the last pilgrimage of Haj, the Prophet told his wives to remain in retirement after his death. Sawda religiously followed this and never went out of the house, even for Haj or Umrah,[9] though all other wives except Zaynab, used to go out.

Generosity was the common characteristic of all the wives of the Prophet that they had learnt from the Prophet himself. Sawda was one who always practiced generosity. It is believed that she used to prepare leather from skins brought from Tart and used to give the money to charity. Once, Umar had sent a purse full of dirhams to her. She immediately distributed all of it to the needy and the poor.[10]

Sawda was slightly short tempered although she had a good sense of humour. When Muslim women were not directed to cover themselves, the wives of the Prophet used to go out to answer the call of nature. Once Umar recognized Sawda and said, "I see, it is you Sawda". She resented this and spoke to the Prophet. It was after this that the Revelation of Quran asking Muslim women to observe purdah (Hijab) came.

It is believed that the Prophet once wanted to divorce her. When she came to know this, she was greatly upset. She ran to the Prophet and begged him, "O Messenger of Allah, I wish no worldly things, I will sacrifice my time allocated to me, if you do not want to visit me, but please do not deprive me of being your wife. The Prophet agreed and did not divorce her. She died in 22 or 23 AH. She was buried at Jannat ul Baqui in Madina. She was seventy-two years old at the time of her death. She had one son by name Abdur Rahman from her first husband, who was killed in the Battle of Jalula and became a martyr. She had the honor of being the mother of a martyr.

Aisha Bint Abu Bakr

1.	Parents name	Father: Abdullah Abu Bakr Mother: Umm Rooman
2.	Age at the time of marriage	6 or 7 years 9 or 10 when she joined Prophet
3.	Prophet's age at the time of marriage	51 years
4.	Marital status	Never Married
5.	Children with the previous husbands	None
6.	Children from the Prophet	None
7.	Age at the time of death	63 years
8.	Companionship with the Prophet	10 years
9.	Period of widowhood	44 years
10.	Number of traditions ascribed to her	2,210
11.	Buried at	Madina – Jannat ul Baqui

Aisha (Ayesha) was her name, Siddiqah and Humaira, were her alias names. Her father was Abu Bakr Siddiqh whose real name was Abdullah. Her mother was Umm Rooman bint Aamir. She was the second wife of Abu Bakr. She had a son Abdur Rahman and a daughter, Aisha. There is a difference of opinion about the date of birth of Aisha. Most of the historians agree that she was born in the 3rd or 4th year of Prophethood. Thus, at the time of her marriage, she was six or seven years old and when the marriage was consummated she was nine or ten year's old.[11]

It is believed that after the death of the Prophet's first wife, Khadijah, the Prophet dreamt of a man carrying something in a piece of silk. The man told him, "This is your wife, so uncover her". The Prophet lifted the silk and there was Aisha. The Prophet simply said to himself, "If this be from God, He will bring it to pass". A few nights later, again he saw the same dream, but this time an Angel was carrying that bundle. The Prophet lifted the silk and there was Aisha, he again said to himself, "If this be from God, He will bring it to pass."[12]The Prophet did not tell anything about his dream to anyone, not even to Abu Bakr, but when Khawla, wife of Uthman bin Mazun made a mention of Aisha as a possible wife, he immediately agreed.

When Khawla approached Abu Bakr for his daughter Aisha, he was hesitant on account of two things. He was under the impression that since the Prophet was his brother in faith, he could not marry his daughter to him. However, the Prophet ruled out that argument. Secondly, Mut'im bin Adi had already proposed her for his son Jubair but when Abu Bakr approached Mut'im bin Adi, he agreed to forgo his son's marriage to Aisha. Aisha was married to the Prophet in the month of Shawwal, after his marriage with Sawda. Since she had not reached the age of puberty, she stayed with her father for another three years. After the Prophet had migrated to Madina, he got the Mosque constructed and adjacent to it were two apartments, one for Sawda and another for Aisha.

The Prophet had sent Zayd to get his family - Sawda, his wife, and his two daughters Umm Kulthum and Fatima - to Madina. Abu Bakr also sent word to his son Abdullah to bring his wife and daughters, Asma and Aisha. Aisha was put up with her parents. Due to a change in climate, both Abu Bakr and Aisha fell sick. After their recovery, Abu Bakr wanted the Prophet to take Aisha to his house. The Prophet was hesitant, as he did not have money to give dower. Abu Bakr offered him a loan of 500 dirhams, which the Prophet gave to Aisha. [13]

The marriage took place in the month of Shawwal although this month was considered inauspicious in Arabia since there was once a plague in this month. The Prophet wanted to remove this superstition from the minds of the people. The marriage ceremony was very simple. Aisha was playing with her friends, when she was called by her mother and afterwards sent to a room where some Ansar women were sitting. This was later on followed by the entry of the Prophet in the room. No feast took place. The Prophet was offered a cup of milk, which was shared with Aisha. Aisha herself had described her marriage. She narrated that "I was playing on a see saw and my long streaming hair had become dishevelled. They came and took me from my game and made me ready". They dressed her in a wedding dress made from fine red striped cloth from Bahrain [14] and then her mother took her to the newly built house of the Prophet.

Her marriage did not change her playful ways. Her young friends continued to come to play with her. The Prophet never objected to her playing with her friends. In fact, he used to encourage them. In Aisha's own words "I would be playing with my dolls with the girls, who were my friends, and the Prophet would come in and they would slip out of the house and he would go out after them and bring them back, for he was pleased for my sake to have them there".

Aisha, although very young, had a unique personality. She was exceptionally attractive, charming and graceful, but her greatest quality was her quick wit and sharp memory, she was able to narrate many incidents of her childhood in minute details. She had spent about ten years of her life with the Prophet. Due to her sharp memory and observant nature, she remembered with clarity all that she saw and heard. It is not surprising that Aisha gave a great deal of the knowledge that we have today about the Prophet and the Hadis.

When she opened her eyes, she found herself in a pure Islamic environment, her father, mother and sister praying all the time and reciting verses from the Holy Quran. She used to boast that among the Prophet's wives, she was the only one who had this privilege. It was perhaps her childhood atmosphere that was responsible for her great interest in religion and history. Once, when she was playing with her friends, she had a horse with wings and when the Prophet pointed out how a horse could have wings she immediately related by giving the example of the horse of Sulaiman.[15] This shows her intelligence and sharpness of mind.

Her father, Abu Bakr, was a person of extraordinary intelligence and learning. She had inherited many qualities from him. Like her father, she acquired a good knowledge of history, language and poetry. There is a difference of opinion on the question whether she knew how to read and write, as literacy was practically nil among the Arabs. [16] She was very courageous and outspoken. She was not afraid to talk back in order to find out the truth. Whenever she beat someone in an argument, the Prophet would simply say, "She is the daughter of Abu Bakr, I have not seen anyone more eloquent than Aisha".

The Event Of Ifk (False accusation).

Whenever the Prophet used to go to war, he used to take one of his wives. When he was going to fight the Banu-al-Mustaliq, the lot fell in favor of Aisha. At sunset, they halted for a short while at a place which had no water. Aisha suddenly noticed that the onyx necklace that she was wearing had slipped off some where on the ground. Aisha did not want to go back without the necklace since it was dark, it could not be searched.[17] The Prophet ordered to set up camp there until daylight. This order was not taken well and many complained about the lack of water. It was thought that they would not be able to pray in the morning, as there was no water for ablution. In the last hour of the night, the verse of earth purification was revealed to the Prophet.[18]

If you find no water then purify yourself with clean
earth, wiping here with your face and your hands.
Al- Maidah: 5:6

The next morning, the necklace was found beneath Aisha's camel.

Before they could reach Madina, they again halted at one place. Again the necklace slipped off from her neck.[19] It was at a time when the order for the march had already been given and Aisha had come to sit in her howdah. When she realized that her necklace was missing, she immediately got down and went in search of it. When she returned, much to her surprise, everybody had left. It was presumed that she was in the howdah and as she was so light, the men carrying the howdah did not realize Aisha's absence. Aisha, who trusted Allah, sat down and waited, and was hoping that someone would notice her absence. As she was waiting, she fell asleep. Fortunately, a young Muslim by name Safwan ibn-al Mu'attal, who was following the Army on Prophet's instruction (to see if they dropped anything behind) saw her. He recognized Aisha, as he had seen her before the order of Hijab was given by God. He loudly recited *"Inna lillahi wa innailayi rajiun"*. On hearing this Aisha got up. Without saying a word, he brought his camel near Aisha who sat on it. He followed her on foot, thinking that they would soon catch up with the army, but it was only the next morning that they could enter Madina. Unfortunately, some hypocrites who had seen Safwan and Aisha returning together began to gossip and spread slanderous lies about them. Eventually the story reached the Prophet himself and by then the whole community was talking about what might or might not have happened.

After some time, Aisha fell ill. By this time, the slander was being repeated everywhere but Aisha was unaware of it. The Prophet was very tense. He could neither accept it, nor deny it, especially as he did not have concrete evidence. He was disturbed and did not know what to do. One could understand the tremendous amount of tension through which he was passing. The ringleader of the hypocrites was one Abdullah bin Ubai, who was in league with the Jews. One day the Prophet went to the Mosque and having prayed to God he said, "O people, what do you say of men who injure me with regard to my family, reporting that which is not true.

By God, I know nothing but good of my household and not but good of the man they speak of". Then he said "Ye Muslims, which of you can see justice done to me against the man who has put me in agony concerning my honor".[20] The Prophet's words gave rise to a hot dialogue between the two groups, who were prepared to come to blows. The situation was controlled with great difficulty.

The Prophet was greatly perturbed, but did not know what to do. He asked the advice of Ali and Usamah bin Zayd. Usamah said he did not know anything bad about Aisha. Ali, because of his close relations and the anxiety to relieve the Prophet, advised him that there was no dearth of women for him. This was wrongly interpreted by many and created ill feelings between Aisha and Ali. Ali also advised the Prophet to ask the maidservant about Aisha. When the maidservant was questioned, she openly said that she saw nothing except good in her. The Prophet also asked Zaynab and in spite of the rivalry between the two wives she came out with the truth that she had not seen anything bad in Aisha.

While Aisha was sick, she was unaware of the whisperings going around. She was surprised at the cold behavior of the Prophet who used to come to her to ask about her health. She missed the loving attention that he had shown her in her past illness. Aisha was deeply hurt by his behavior but her ego did not permit her to ask the Prophet for his cold behavior. She simply asked his permission to go to her parent's house.

Even in her parent's house, nobody told her anything. One day, when she went out in the evening with one of her relatives (Mistah's mother), she hinted at what was going on in the city. Aisha was greatly perturbed. She went home and wept for two nights. She did not know that the Prophet had defended her in the Mosque. She was under the impression that the Prophet doubted her character.

The next day the Prophet came and sat down near her and told her "O Aisha I have been told such a thing concerning you. If you are innocent and if you have not done any wrong, surely God will declare thine innocence, and if you have done wrong, then ask for forgiveness of God and repent to Him, for verily if the slave confesses his sin and then repent, God forgives him". Aisha on hearing this started weeping and asked her parents to answer on her behalf, but both of them said we do not know what to say. Then she herself mustered courage and said, "What am I to say. If I told you that I committed, which I did not commit, you would believe me, but if I deny it, you would not believe me. I shall only say to you what Yaqub, the father of Yusuf said: lovely patience and God is the one whose help is to be sought in relation to your allegations". [21]

Aisha hoped that God would declare her innocence but she never expected that a Revelation would come. When all of them were sitting, suddenly the Prophet started having the signs of a Revelation. When he was relieved of that pressure, he happily announced, "O Aisha, praise God for He hath declared thee innocent". On hearing that, her parents asked her to thank the Messenger of Allah but she was adamant. She said, "I will not rise to go to him and I will praise none but God".

The Revelation was:

Surely those who concocted the slander one from a clique among you. Do not regard this incident as only an evil, for it also contains a good lesson for you. Whoever took any part in this sin has took on him the leading part, shall have a terrible punishment. Why did not the believing men and believing women, when they heard of this slander, think well of their own people and say this is clearly a false accusation
An-Nur: 24:11,12.

The Revelation gave great relief to all the people. Muslims were jubilant but no punishment was given to the evil mongers.

The Incident of Ila

The Prophet was a true embodiment of Quranic teachings. He used to live a very simple life. His wives, although occupying extra ordinary positions, were deprived of all the luxuries of life. In Madina, after establishing the Islamic State, the economic position of the state improved. The Prophet distributed bounties to many people, but did not keep anything for his family. Most of his wives were from well to do families and had all the comforts of life but now they were put to great hardship. Naturally, some of the wives felt bad and demanded some extra allowance for them.

One day, when Umar came to the Prophet, he heard the sound of women's voices at a high pitch. He was taken a back, as he had not expected the Prophet's wives to talk so rudely to him. This situation considerably disturbed the Prophet. He declared that he would not go to his wives for a month. Also, the Prophet had a fall from a horse, resulting in an injury to his leg and he had to retire in a room isolated from his wives. This gave rise to the suspicion that the Prophet had divorced all his wives. Umar was extremely perturbed on this issue and when he met the Prophet after waiting for a long time, the first question he asked was, "Have you divorced your wives?" He was extremely happy when he got the answer in the negative. All the people were relieved of the tension that had caused a gloomy atmosphere.

Aisha was the third wife of the Prophet. Since Khadijah had died and Sawda was an elderly lady, who acted more like a caretaker of the house, Aisha got all the attention and love of the Prophet. The Prophet who was starving for love after Khadijah's death, found in Aisha an embodiment of love and affection. Aisha was not a stranger to him. Everyday he used to go to Abu Bakr's house. He had seen her from her birth and played with her. Despite her young age, she had a profound understanding of the needs of her husband who was leading a chequered life full of great dangers and troubles. However, Aisha could not enjoy the same pivotal position forever. Gradually, other wives entered the household. After Aisha, he married eight more wives and every time she felt an encroachment on her sphere of love. When the Prophet married Hafsah, the daughter of Umar, Aisha could compromise with her, as there was not much difference of age between the two. Soon, both became good friends. However, Zaynab's entry into the household created great tension for her since she was the only one who used to compare herself with Aisha on account of her close relationship with the Prophet and also because her marriage was performed by God. She always thought that she had an edge over Aisha.

Aisha was always protective of her rights and did not like the Prophet to spend more time with Zaynab, as was evident from the incident of honey, after which an Ayah was revealed warning the two girls, though not by name (Pl. refer to the chapter, Prophet As A Husband for a detailed account). Safiyah, the Jewish wife of the Prophet was also very beautiful. Safiyah loved the Prophet very much and this naturally was the cause of Aisha's jealousy. When Maria, the Coptic slave girl, came into the life of the Prophet and had a son from her, Aisha became more envious. One day, when the Prophet brought Ibrahim, his son, to Aisha's place and told her that he was so much like him, Aisha replied, "I don't see any likeness". Then the Prophet said, "Don't you see how fair his skin is"? And again she replied, "All those who are fed on so much milk are plump and fair skinned". [22] Aisha as a woman was bound to have such feelings because even though she was young, she did not have any child. These feelings of envy were a natural phenomenon. For everyone, the center of attraction was the Prophet. Every wife was deeply in love with him, so it was not easy to share this love with some other person.

It is related from Aisha, that the Prophet once told her, "O Aisha, this is Gabriel who gives you the greeting". She replied "Peace be upon him and the mercy of Allah and His blessings". When Umar was badly wounded and he knew that he was going to die, he sent his son to Aisha requesting her if he could be buried near the Prophet. Aisha had kept that place for herself, but realizing the great honor that he had done to her, she gave him preference. This was of course a great sacrifice on Aisha's part who would have loved to be near the Prophet even after his death.

Aisha was sick for sometime and died on 17th Ramadan, 59 AH (June 678 AD.) She was 63 years old. She had survived 44 years after the death of the Prophet. The only wife who was alive at that time was Umm Salamah. Aisha was buried in Jannatul Baqui, where all the other wives of the Prophet were buried. She willed that she should be buried the same night, so accordingly her burial took place after Isha prayers, which were attended, by a large number of people.

Aisha was an extremely generous lady. Whatever money she used to get, she used to distribute it among the poor and the needy. Umar had fixed 12,000 dirhams annually for her but the moment she used to get the money, she had it distributed within hours. This only shows how indifferent she was towards the material things of life.

Aisha's contribution in consolidating and spreading the message of the Prophet and the Quran was extra ordinary. Although she lived with the Prophet only for about ten years, she had quoted 2,210 traditions that are the most authentic. She rendered the greatest service to the community after the death of the Prophet for 44 years as a widow. She was the most learned and scholarly person of her time in the knowledge of Quran, the fundamentals of religion, fiqh, poetry and medicine. During his lifetime, the Prophet himself had acknowledged Aisha's mastery over the subjects. It is reported that the Prophet used to direct Muslims to make use of her erudition saying, "Take your lessons from this Humayra". [23]After the death of the Prophet, many a time, people used to quote the Prophet out of context, changing the meaning of his message. In such cases, she always used to correct them and explain to them the proper meaning, with the result that even Caliph used to send people to her to get the correct picture. Aisha used to go to Haj practically every year. The idea behind this was that she was able to meet thousands of people and extend the message of the Prophet.They were many who wanted clarifications from her on different issues.

A number of authorities have testified the scholarship of Aisha. Imam az Zuhri of At Tabiun said that Aisha was the most learned among the Muslims - Many learned companions of the Prophet consulted her. Urwah ibn az Zubayr said that Aisha was the most scholarly person in the sciences of the Quran, Poetry, Fiqh, Medicine, History of the Arabs and their Genealogy. She was ranked with Abdullah ibn Abbas, Ali bin Abu Talib, Umar bin Khattab and Abdullah bin Masud among the five most learned Muslim companions of the Prophet. [24]

She used to conduct classes at home. On her recommendation, the Prophet had allotted certain days for women to talk to him to seek clarifications on most points. Even after the passing away of the Prophet, this practice continued and Aisha used to provide guidance to women. She was keenly interested in the education and training of children. There were a number of boys and girls under her patronage. Thus, she silently tried to bring about social change through an army of young, devoted Muslims. She had taken the responsibility for maintenance of many girls and arranged their marriages. In one of the marriages of an Ansar girl, the ceremony was very simple. When the Prophet came inside, he asked Aisha, "where is the music?"[25] It only shows that music and singing were allowed in Islam with certain restrictions.

Aisha used to say that she had an edge over the other wives due to the following reasons. She was born in a Muslim family; her father, mother, sister and brother were all Muslims. This was not the privilege of any other wife of the Prophet. She had listened to the recitation of the Quran from her childhood and had even memorized it. Gabriel brought her picture to the Prophet and said that she was his wife. Her father Abu Bakr was a very learned man. He was the closest companion of the Prophet and the Prophet always used to praise him. She was the only one who did not marry anyone else before marrying to Prophet.Good part of the Revelations came when the Prophet was in her apartment. Her innocence was testified by God through a Revelation. She was the most beloved wife and the Prophet in front of many people admitted this. Before his death, the Prophet preferred to stay in her apartment and ultimately died in her lap. He was also buried in her apartment.

Aisha's role is also of great significance in appreciating the role of Muslim women in an Islamic society. In spite of the fact that the wives of the Prophet had to observe *Pardah* (Hijab) and even wear a veil, there was no strict segregation between the sexes. Muslim women were allowed to take part in public affairs.Aisha not only accompanied the Prophet in many wars but also helped in serving the wounded warriors. Over and above this, she led the battle of the Camel. She had no intention of fighting against Ali. She actually went to establish peace, but her presence on the battlefield was misunderstood. Aisha's role proved that there was no field that was restricted for women. Women could do anything that was not prohibited by religion. It was only centuries later that undesirable restrictions were placed on women. Aisha was broad-minded and visionary. In those days the *Gilaf* (cover) of the Kabah was changed every year, and to avoid disrespect it was buried. On Aisha's advice, it was cut into pieces and sold to the people instead of being buried. This added not only money to the public exchequer but put an end to an undesirable practice.

It is not easy to make a correct assessment of Aisha's immense contribution to the Muslim community. Most significant was her part in the preservation of the Ahadis (traditions of the Prophet). As a teacher of the Islamic precepts, she created a cadre of scholars who later on spread out to convey the message of the revolutionary new religion. Her contribution to the Arabic literature of the day was also notable. She entered the house of the Prophet when she was still a young girl. Yet she was mentally mature enough to handle adroitly the responsibility of taking care of a much older person, a leader charged with the responsibility of conveying the Message of God. The Prophet was very happy when he was in her company.

It was so pathetic to think of a young girl of 18 or 19 becoming a widow and then spending a long period of about 44 years as a widow without the support of her close relatives. First, she lost her mother, and then a few years after the Prophet's death, she lost her father. She had no children. Although a second marriage was common in Arab society, she was prohibited from marrying again as God had prohibited the remarrying of the Prophet's wives.

Aisha spent her whole life after her husband in the cause of Islam, educating people, both men and women in various aspects of the new faith. She concentrated her efforts in achieving propagation of the message of Islam. She was selected by God, to serve as the wife of the Prophet and enhance the knowledge of Islam. The traditions of the Prophet recorded by her are regarded by all scholars as the most authentic. She had a photographice memory.

Her thirst for knowledge and truth made her the most learned woman of her time. She surpassed men in many fields of knowledge. Her wit made her one of the most eloquent speakers among her contemporaries. Her dedication to the cause of Islam has kept inspiring young girls of succeeding generations. She was a role model among women in developing a progressive Muslim society.

Hafsah Bint Umar Khattab

1.	Parents name	Father: Umar bin Khattab Mother: Zaynab bin Maz`um
2.	Age at the time of marriage	20 years
3.	Prophet's age at the time of marriage	54 years
4.	Marital status	Widow
5.	Children with the previous husbands	None
6.	Children with the prophet	None
7.	Age at the time of death	59 years
8.	Companionship with the Prophet	9 years
9.	Period of widowhood	30 years
10.	Number of traditions ascribed to her	60
11.	Buried at	Madina – Jannat ul Baqui

Hafsah was the daughter of Umar bin Khattab. Her mother was Zaynab bin Mazum. In the early period of Prophethood, Umar was a formidable opponent of Islam, but after he embraced Islam, he became one of its sturdiest pillars. He was known for his forceful personality and uncanny courage. Throughout his life, he was very protective of the Prophet. He rose to become the second Caliph.

Hafsah was first married to Khunais son of Huzaifa from the tribe of Banu Salaam. Husband and wife both migrated to Abyssinia in the second batch. Khunais fought the battle of Badr in which he was badly wounded and could not survive. Umar was worried and wanted to get her married. He approached Uthman, whose wife Ruqayya – Prophet's daughter - had just died. Uthman was not in a mood to marry, so he politely refused. Then Umar approached Abu Bakr, who also did not respond positively to the proposal. Umar became very upset and narrated the episode to the Prophet. The Prophet told him "I will show you a better son- in-law than Uthman, and I will show him a better father-in-law than you".[26]On hearing this, Umar smiled and understood the meaning of the sentence. Afterwards, Abu Bakr told him the reason for his indifference to Umar's proposal, since he had a feeling that the Prophet had the intention of marrying Hafsah. The Prophet got his daughter Umm Kulthum, married to Uthman and he himself married Hafsah. A third apartment was built for her, adjacent to the Mosque.

Hafsah was first married at a very early age and became a widow when she was 18 years old. At the time of her marriage with the Prophet she was about 20. She had inherited qualities of her father's strong personality, who also was an outstanding jurist and a great social reformer. She had inherited his courage and the other qualities of his head and heart. She was good at reading and writing. The Prophet had given special attention to her skills and appointed a teacher to help her. In her thirst for knowledge she was next only to Aisha. The written copy of the Quran which was recorded by Zyad Ibn Thabit on Abu Bakr's instructions was given to Umar. Umar then gave it to Hafsah for safekeeping. When Uthman became the Caliph he instructed that this copy of the Quran be used to make severel copies for distribution.[28] Hafsah used to discuss various religious and social issues with the Prophet. The Prophet also took keen interes, in discussions with her with the result that she became a very good teacher, guide and an authority on various topics concerning the new faith. Knowing her curiosity, the Prophet asked Shifa, to teach Hafsah the cure of insect bites—a field in which Shifa was regarded as an authority. [29]

Hafsah was a very religious woman. She remained dedicated to prayers and fasting, till the end of her life. She also memorized Quran.Hafsah was a little short tempered and assertive. She did not have much patience, especially while discussing matters with the Prophet. She would go on arguing with the Prophet, many a time in a loud voice. Her father did not like her behavior, and often warned her against it.

Hafsah and Aisha were good friends. Both were jealous of other wives. Once, both of them made a plot against the Prophet, but God did not like this and warned them, though not by name. It is reported that once the Prophet wanted to divorce Hafsah, but Gabriel came with a divine command and informed him that Hafsah was one of his wives in paradise.[30]

Hafsah died in 45 AH at the age of 59. Before her death, she asked her brother Abdullah bin Umar to distribute her property to the poor. She had no children. She quoted 60 traditions. She was buried in Janatul Baqui, in Madina.

Zaynab Bint Khuzayamah
Umm-ul-Masakeen

1.	Parents name	Father: Kuzamayah bin Harith
2.	Age at the time of marriage	30 years
3.	Prophet's age at the time of marriage	55 years
4.	Marital status	Widow, married thrice
5.	Children with the previous husbands	None
6.	Children with the prophet	None
7.	Age at the time of death	30 years
8.	Companionship with the Prophet	A few months
9.	Period of widowhood	None
10.	Number of traditions ascribed to her	None
11.	Buried at	Madina – Jannat ul Baqui

Zaynab was the daughter of Khuzayamah bin Harith, who belonged to the Bedouin tribe of Amir. There are divergent reports about her previous husbands. According to one report she was first married to Abdullah bin Jahsh who was killed in the battle of Uhud. According to another report, she was first married to Tufail ibnul al Harith and when divorced by him was remarried to his brother Ubaidah ibnul Harith, Muhammad's cousin who was killed in the battle of Badr.[31] He was a very devoted and brave Muslim. During the social boycott, he was with the Prophet and it is presumed that Zaynab, his wife, must have also been with him sharing the trial and tribulations of those days. He prayed that he should die fighting for Islam. His desire was fulfilled and he died in the battle of Badr. After his death, she was married to Abdullah bin Jahsh who was also a devoted Muslim.[32] First he migrated to Abyssinia then to Madina. He was also the cousin brother of the Prophet. He also wished that he should die in the cause of Islam. His desire was also fulfilled. He died while fighting bravely in the battle of Uhad. He was buried in the graveyard of Uhad where Prophet's uncle Hamza.was also buried.[33]

The Prophet was aware of the sacrifice that Zaynab had made in the cause of Islam. In spite of all the hardship; she was a staunch devotee of the Prophet.It was but natural for a softhearted person like the Prophet to support her and safeguard her interest. It was this consideration that prompted him to accept her as his wife. The marriage took place in the month of Ramadan, 3 AH. The Prophet gave her 400 dirhams. She was thirty years old at the time of marriage. A fourth apartment, adjacent to the Mosque was built for her. The Prophet could not enjoy the company of this great lady for long as she died within a few months after the marriage. She was the only fortunate wife whose funeral prayer was performed by the Prophet, as at the time of Khadijah's death the Prophet had not received the divine command regarding funeral prayers. She was also buried in Jannat-ul-Baqui.

She had an extremely generous nature. She used to listen to the talk of poor and needy people. It was due to her great concern for the poor that she earned the title of Umm-ul-Masakeen (the mother of the poor) even before she got married to the Prophet. Once there was nothing to eat except a little flour, when a beggar asked her for food, she gave that away and went without food. The Prophet was greatly touched by this act of generosity and got her food from the neighbor's house. The next morning, he narrated this to his other wives and said, "If you put your trust in God, He would provide for your sustenance even as He does for the birds".

Umm Salamah Bint Abi Umayya

1.	Parents name	Father: Abi Umayya al Makhazamiyah Mother: Atika bint Amr
2.	Age at the time of marriage	29 years
3.	Prophet's age at the time of marriage	56 years
4.	Marital status	Widow
5.	Children with the previous husbands	4
6.	Children with the prophet	None
7.	Age at the time of death	84 years
8.	Companionship with the Prophet	7 years
9.	Period of widowhood	48 years
10.	Number of traditions ascribed to her	378
11.	Buried at	Madina – Jannat ul Baqui

Umm Salamah's father was Abi Ummayah al-Makhazumi Yah. Her mother was Atika bint Amr. Her name was Hind, but she was known as Umm Salamah. Her father was very rich and generous. He used to feed the travellers, and was known as *Zad ar-Rakib* (the one who provides food to travellers) .Umm Salamah had all the luxuries of life as she belonged to a very rich family. She was also very beautiful. She was married to Abu Salamah who was the Prophet's nephew. The same slave girl of Abu Lahab, called Thuwaiba who had nursed the Prophet in the beginning also nursed him. Due to this relationship, there was great affection between the Prophet and Abu Salamah.

Umm Salamah and her husband loved each other very much. Once she wanted to make a pact that if one dies, the other will not marry again, but Abu Salamah told her that if he died first, she should marry again and prayed to God to grant Umm Salamah after me a man who will cause her no sadness and no hurt".[34] Umm Salamah used to wonder who could be a better person than her husband. It was only when she got married to the Prophet that she realized the truth of her husband's prayer.

Umm Salamah and Abu Salamah were very sincere and devoted to the cause of Islam. They belonged to the earlier batch that had accepted Islam. When the torture to Muslims by the Quraish became unbearable, the Prophet advised them to migrate to Abyssinia. They belonged to the first batch of migrants. The King of Abyssinia was a noble man, but the Quraish were displeased with his act and approached the King to withdraw his support to the refugees. The King had a detailed discussion with the representatives of the Quraish and ultimately he was convinced that he was right in giving protection to the Meccan refugees. He turned down the request of the Quraish and sent them back. Umm Salamah had witnessed the whole conversation between the two. Her description of what transpired is considered a historic document of great value.

The couple returned to Mecca on being incorrectly informed that the Quraish had embraced Islam. As they were somewhat scared to enter the city, they sought the protection of Abu Talib, who was Abu Salamah's maternal uncle. Both husband and wife were very close to the Prophet. On the occasion of the marriage of the Prophet's daughter, Fatima, the couple helped in making arrangements. Umm Salamah, along with Aisha, went to make the house ready for the couple and to prepare the food. Aisha would have never dreamt that she would become her competitor one day.

When Muslims started migrating to Madina, she was the first woman to join them but the story of her migration was pathetic. When she was going along with her husband and young son to Madina, the families of both Umm Salamah and Abu Salamah tried to stop them. Umm Salamah's parents did not want her to move to Madina along with her husband, so they dragged her away. As Abu Salamah was alone, he was subdued. On seeing this, the people from Abu Salamah's side, snatched the boy from the hands of his mother. With great difficulty Abu Salamah, escaped and reached Madina. Umm Salamah was very upset and grieved as she was separated both from her husband and son. For one year, every day she used to go to the place where she was separated from her family and cry. One day, one of her cousins was moved by her pathetic condition and requested her parents to let her join her husband. Her parents agreed. Her husband's family also gave her son back to her. Umm Salamah decided to go alone with her son to Madina. As she was riding the camel alone, she was recognized by Osman bin Abi Talah, who was an enemy of Islam. However, he was so much moved by the devotion, faith and courage of Umm Salamah, that he accompanied her, walking all the way to Madina. When Madina came near, he stopped and asked her to join her husband. Umm Salamah said that she had not seen a man more pious than Osman.

Abu Salamah was a very courageous warrior. He fought very bravely in the battle of Badr, but in the battle of Uhad he was seriously injured and after sometime he died in 4 AH. Umm Salamah herself came to the Prophet to inform him of the sad demise of her husband. The Prophet immediately went to her house. He led his funeral prayer and unusually called *"Allahu Akbar"* nine times. When asked why he exceeded the limit, the Prophet said he deserved a thousand.[35] When the Prophet went to offer condolences to the widow, he said, pray to God to give you a better person. Umm Salamah used to think who could be a better person than her beloved husband.

At the time of her husband's death, she was pregnant. After delivery when her days of *Iddat* were over, it is believed that Abu Bakr and Umar both sent the proposal to marry her, but she refused. Even when the Prophet offered to marry her, she did not accept in the first instance. She feared that she was not a suitable match for the Prophet. "I am a woman whose best time hath gone and I am a mother of orphans. What is more, I have a nature of exceeding jealousy and thou, O Messenger of God, hast already more than one wife." The Prophet replied "As to the age I am older than thou, as to the jealousy, I will pray to God to take it from thee, as to the orphan children, God and His Messenger will take care of them."[36] Ultimately she agreed and they were married in Shawwal in 4 AH. She was lodged in the house that had earlier belonged to the late Zaynab.

Despite what she had said about her age, Umm Salamah was still in her youth. She was about 29 years old. She was only 18 years old when she migrated to Abyssinia. As regards the point about her jealousy, she was quite right. Aisha had accepted Hafsah and even Zaynab but with Umm Salamah it was different. Every one in Madina was praising the beauty of Umm Salamah. Aisha was troubled and apprehensive. In her own words, "I was grievously sad, for what they told me of her beauty so I made myself agreeable to her that I may observe her closely and I saw that she was many times more beautiful than they had said".[37]

Umm Salamah was a learned lady. She used to listen keenly to the Prophet's discourses and remembered quite a few of them. She had to her credit 378 traditions.[38] She was an authority on Fatwa (verdict in Islamic jurisprudence). She also led the prayers of ladies. She used to fast three days in a week – Monday, Thursday and Friday. She was very regular in her Tahajjud (mid-night) prayers. She also memorized Quran.

She was greatly in love with the Prophet. She had kept a few hair of the Prophet in a small silver box. When people used to come to her with sufferings, she used to put these hairs in a glass of water and people used to get relief by drinking that water out of their great faith in the Prophet.[39] Once she was wearing a necklace, which had some gold in it, when the Prophet saw it he just looked at the necklace but did not say anything. She realized that he did not like it and immediately took it out. It is said that she broke it. Umm Salamah was also a very good cook. On the very first day of her marriage she prepared a dish for the Prophet.

Umm Salamah played a significant role in supporting the Prophet. When the treaty of Hudaybiyah was signed, many people were not happy with the conditions put forward by the Quraish. They were also upset, as they were not allowed to do Umrah that year and they had to return without performing Umrah. When the Prophet asked them to get their heads shaved and sacrifice their animals, they did not want to follow these rituals since they had not performed Umrah. The Prophet became very disturbed on the issue, as his followers were always ready to abide by his orders. It was at this point that Umm Salamah gave a very sound advice to the Prophet to go ahead without caring for others. When the Prophet shaved his head and sacrificed an animal, automatically others followed him, and an ugly situation was avoided.[40]

Once, after the death of the Prophet, she saw him in her dream. He was very sad, his hair were full of dust. She asked him what the matter was and he said that Hussain had been martyred. Umm Salamah got up and then she got the news of Hussain's death .Umm Salamah narrated that once she was sitting with Maymonah, the other wife of the Prophet, when Abdullah Maktum came to see the Prophet. The Prophet asked them to observe Hijab, they said "but he is a blind man". The Prophet replied "but you are not".

Umm Salamah had four children from her first husband. Once she asked the Prophet, whether she would get rewarded if she spent the money on them, the Prophet said "surely" She was the last of his wives to die. She was eighty-four years old at the time of her death. Hazrat Abuharira led her funeral prayer. She was also buried in Jannat-ul-Baqui.

Zaynab Bint Jah`sh

1.	Parents name	Father: Jah`sh bin Riyat Mother: Umayma
2.	Age at the time of marriage	34 years
3.	Prophet's age at the time of marriage	57 years
4.	Marital status	Divorced
5.	Children with the previous husbands	None
6.	Children with the Prophet	None
7.	Age at the time of death	53 years
8.	Companionship with the Prophet	6 years
9.	Period of widowhood	13 years
10.	Number of traditions ascribed to her	11
11.	Buried at	Madina – Jannat ul Baqui

Zaynab's father was Jah'sh bin Riyab. Her mother was Umayma, the daughter of Abdul Muttalib, who was the grand father of the Prophet. As such she was the first cousin of the Prophet. She belonged to the tribe of Quraish. She was an early convert and had migrated to Madina along with the Prophet.

The Prophet wanted her to get married to Zayd, his adopted son. This was in addition to his first wife Umm Ayman, who was the Prophet's nurse and was much older to him.[41] Now the Prophet wanted Zayd to marry Zaynab a woman of his age. Another reason was perhaps to eliminate the distinction between the slave and the master, and to treat all on equal footing. But Zaynab did not like this proposal as she considered Zayd of inferior lineage, which was not true. Zayd's parents were from the tribes of Bani Kalb and Bani Tavy, which in no way were inferior to Bani Asad, to which Zaynab's parents belonged. Moreover, till that time he was known as Zayd bin Muhammad.

In Islam, all are equal. There is no distinction between master and servant and God wanted to convey this message to the people. He wanted this marriage to be solemnized, so he revealed an Ayah after which Zaynab had no choice but to accept the proposal.

> ### *It is not fitting for a believing man or a believing woman to have an option in their affairs when a matter has been decided by Allah and His Rasool*
> ### *Al-Ahzab : 33 : 36*

At the time of her marriage with Zayd, she was about thirty-four years old. It was reported that she was quite beautiful. It was not very clear whether it was her first or second marriage. Historians seem to be unclear on this issue. Doubt arises because in Arabia, of that time girls were usually married at a very early age and it was a surprise that Zaynab, who was beautiful and belonged to a respectable family, had remained unmarried till the age of thirty-four. Ibn Sa'd in his book Tabaquat narrated a tradition from Usman, the nephew of Zaynab. It is stated that when the Prophet sent her the proposal to marry Zayd, she argued, "I do not like him because I am a widow from the Quraish family".[42]

Before this marriage, Zayd was living with the Prophet as a member of his family but after his marriage with Zaynab, the Prophet arranged a separate house for the couple.[43] They could hardly live together for a year or so. There was always tension in the family due to the superiority complex of Zaynab. Zayd complained to the Prophet a number of times, but the Prophet tried to console him "keep your wife and fear God" once he said to Zayd "of the things listed, the most hateful to God is divorce". In spite of this, Zayd and Zaynab agreed to separate as life had became intolerable for them.

After the divorce, the Prophet wanted to marry Zaynab to do away with the tradition of Quraish that did not admit marriage with the wife of an adopted son. There was already a lot of opposition and people were waiting for a chance to tarnish the Prophet's character. In Arab society, an adopted son was treated as a real son and marrying his wife was taken as marrying one's daughter-in-law. Time passed on, and the Prophet was not able to take any decision. Then the Revelation came

> ### *We gave her to you in marriage, so that there remains no hindrance for the believers to wed the wives of their adopted sons, if they divorced them. And Allah's command had to be carried out*
> ### *Al Ahzab:33:37*

When Zaynab was informed of her marriage with the Prophet, she prostrated before Allah in thanks. As God had already endorsed the marriage, the Prophet gave a feast the next day. It is believed it was one of the finest *walima* feasts given by him. It is reported that Umm Salamah, had sent some Malidah (a sweet dish) for the groom but the Prophet invited everyone present there and everyone ate that.

Among the Prophet's wives only Zaynab could claim parity with Aisha. She used to claim superiority because she was the only one whose marriage was endorsed by God. With the increase in the number of wives, it was not possible to maintain complete harmony among them. On many occasions, the wives were divided into two groups, one led by Aisha followed by Hafsah and Sawda, the other led by Zaynab. It was known to people that Aisha was the beloved wife of the Prophet. People who wanted some favor from the Prophet used to send gifts to him when he used to be with Aisha. They presumed that he would be in his best mood. But the other wives did not like this. They wanted that the Prophet should tell the people to discontinue this practice. The wives tried to convince the Prophet through his daughter Fatima, but failed to achieve the desired result. Then they deputed Zaynab for the task. She boldly and eloquently tried to argue that Aisha did not deserve this privilege.

Zaynab died at the age of 53 years. Before her death, she had selected her shroud and directed that if the Caliph sent another shroud for her, then one of the two may be given to the poor. Her residential house after her death was purchased by the Caliph for 50,000 dirhams, for the extension of the Mosque.[44]

Zaynab was a very pious lady. Umm Salamah is quoted to have said that Zaynab was a good natured, fast keeping and prayer offering person. Even Aisha, who considered her as her rival admitted that, "I have not seen a woman more religious, more generous and more dedicated in the service of God than Zaynab. The only weakness in her was that she was very sensitive but she used to acknowledge her mistakes and repent".

Zaynab was very generous. When Umar sent her annual allowance of 12,000 dirhams, without looking at it, she covered it in a cloth and asked the servant to distribute it to the poor and needy. When the entire amount was distributed, she prayed to God that she did not wish to live any more to be the recipient of Umar's dole. She died the same year.[45]

Once, the Prophet told his wives that the one that had long arms would follow him soon in heaven. The wives used to measure their arms. Sawda had the longest arms. But when Zaynab died after the death of the Prophet, it was understood that by long arms, the Prophet had meant the one who was most generous.

Juwayriah Bint al Harith

1.	Parents name	Father: al-Hārith ibn Abi Dirar:
2.	Age at the time of marriage	20 years
3.	Prophet's age at the time of marriage	57 years
4.	Marital status	Widow
5.	Children with the previous husbands	None
6.	Children with the prophet	None
7.	Age at the time of death	65 years
8.	Companionship with the Prophet	6 years
9.	Period of widowhood	39 years
10.	Number of traditions ascribed to her	7
11.	Buried at	Madina – Jannat ul Baqui

Juwayriah's name was Barrah. She was the daughter of Harith, the Chief of Banu al Mustaliq tribe. This tribe was very much against the Prophet and wanted to harm him. When the Prophet came to know the intention of the Chief of the tribe, he immediately proceeded towards them. In the ensuing battle, Muslims were victorious and the enemies received a crushing defeat. The chief of the tribe, Harith, somehow escaped, but about seventy to eighty people became prisoners. Harith's daughter Barrah, who was about twenty years old, was in that lot of prisoners. She was very beautiful. She came to the lot of an ordinary soldier, Thabit bint Qayas .She did not like to be his captive, so she asked him to fix her ransom so that she can arrange for the money and she may be freed. Knowing that she was the daughter of the chief of the tribe, Thabit bint Qayas fixed a quantity of gold, which was at that time about 4,000 dirhams. In fact, she did not have any money nor she had any source to pay but she had the courage, so she approached the Prophet for intervention. That day the Prophet was in Aisha's apartment when she came there, Aisha, seeing her attractive looks tried her best to send her away without giving her a chance to meet the Prophet. When the two women were standing at the door, the Prophet had a chance to look out of the house and saw the ardent and eager Juwayriah refusing to be sent away.[46]

Juwayriah entered into the apartment and said, "O Messenger of God, I am the daughter of Harith, well, thou knowest the distress that hath fallen upon me and I have come to seek thy help in the matter of my ransom". The Prophet replied "Wouldst thou have better than that?" "What is better?" she asked. The Prophet answered, "That I should pay thy ransom and marry thee." She gladly accepted the offer. But the marriage did not take place immediately. When her father came to know that she had become a captive, he came to the Prophet with camels full of load to pay the ransom. But on his way, he separated two very good camels and hid them somewhere in the valley. He came to the Prophet and said, "O Muhammad, thou hast captured my daughter and here is the ransom". The Prophet asked him "but where are those two camels which thou didst hide in Aqiq?" Harith was astonished, as except God no one knew about this. He said, "I testify that there is no God, but God and thou the Muhammad is the messenger of God"[47]. He and his two sons embraced Islam. There is another tradition that when Harith asked the Prophet to release his daughter after taking the ransom, the Prophet said I leave it to your daughter, but she preferred to be the wife of the Prophet.[48]

The Prophet married her and gave her the dower of 400 dirhams. He kept her in a separate apartment adjacent to the Mosque. He gave her the name Juwayriah. She was already married and her husband Maraf bin Safwan was killed in the battle.

Juwayriah was very beautiful. In the words of Aisha "She was a woman of great loveliness and beauty. No man looked at her but she captivated his soul and when I saw her first at the door of my room I was filled with misgivings for I knew that the Prophet would see in her what I saw".[49]

Juwayriah's marriage was a great blessing for her people, as one hundred families were released from captivity overnight. Aisha remarked "I know no woman who was a greater blessing to her people than she".[50]

After embracing Islam, she became very devoted. Most of the time, she used to spend in prayers. Once the Prophet came to her apartment in the morning and found her praying. When in the afternoon he passed that way, he found her still sitting at the same place and praying. The Prophet asked her if it was her daily routine and she said "yes." She used to fast generally on Thursdays and Fridays. Her sisters and brothers also became Muslims. She died at the age of 65 years. She survived 40 years after the death of the Prophet. She was buried like the other wives in Jannat-ul-Baqui.

Umm Habiba Bint Abu Sufyan

1.	Parents name	Father: Abu Sufyan Sakhar Mother: Safiah bint Abu Aas
2.	Age at the time of marriage	36 years
3.	Prophet's age at the time of marriage	57 years
4.	Marital status	Widow
5.	Children with the previous husbands	2
6.	Children with the prophet	None
7.	Age at the time of death	72 years
8.	Companionship with the Prophet	6 years
9.	Period of widowhood	30 years
10.	Number of traditions ascribed to her	65
11.	Buried at	Madina – Jannat ul Baqui

Umm Habiba's original name was Ramlah. She was the daughter of Abu Sufyan Sakhar, who was a staunch opponent of Islam. Her mother's name was Safiah bint Abu Aas who was the paternal aunt of Hazrat Uthman. Ramlah had a daughter by the name Habiba. She adopted her kunniyat after her daughter's name and was known as Umm Habiba. Although born in a family which was opposed to Islam, she embraced Islam in the early days along with her husband, Ubaydullah bin Jah'sh. The couple migrated to Abyssinia.

Ubaydullah was Christian[51] before he embraced Islam and after their migration to Abyessinia, he again reverted to Christianity. Umm Habiba tried her best to stop him but he went astray. He became a drunkard. This had an adverse effect on his health that ultimately led to his death. In spite of her husband's conversion to Christianity, she remained a Muslim. After her husband's death, there was no one to support her, as she did not have any relative in Abyssinia. Ubayadullah was the Prophet's cousin. When the Prophet came to know of the sad demise, he sent a message to the Negus, the king of Abyssinia, asking him to arrange his marriage with Umm Habiba if she was willing. The Prophet did not send any direct message to her but it is believed that she had a dream in which some one came to her and addressed her as the mother of the faithful and she interpreted this to mean that she would became the wife of the Prophet. The next day, she received the message from Negus through his maidservant Arabaha, asking for her consent and to nominate someone on her behalf to negotiate the marriage. Umm Habiba was so pleased that she rewarded Arabah by offering her silver jewelry.[52]

Negus solemnized the marriage. It was a marriage in absentia as the bridegroom was not present at the time of marriage. Negas gave 400 dinars, (equivalent to 4,000 dirhams) which was the highest dower given to a wife of the Prophet. A feast in his palace followed the wedding and all the Muslims were invited. Negus paid all the expenses of marriage. Shortly afterwards, Negus ordered all the arrangements to be made for Umm Habiba's departure to Madina. The Prophet requested Jafar and other Muslims who had migrated to Abyssinia to return to Madina. Negus arranged for two boats to take the people to Madina.

The Prophet took this decision of marrying Umm Habiba in view of the circumstances prevailing there. Firstly, he was moved by the fate of Umm Habiba, because of her sufferings especially when her husband reverted back to Christianity, but she continued to be a staunch Muslim. He also wanted Negus to help the Muslims in coming back to Madina and lastly he wanted to win over Abu Sufyan, the father of Umm Habiba, who was opposed to Islam but was naturally worried about the fate of his daughter. When Abu Sufyan heard of his daughter's marriage to the Prophet, he said "Muhammad is a person of high caliber against whom no one can say anything bad." He recognized that it was an honor for any one to be related to the Prophet by marriage.[53] When Umm Habiba came to Madina, the Prophet was in Khyber. When he came back, he gave a feast on the occasion of his marriage.

At the time of marriage, Umm Habiba was thirty-six or thirty seven years old. In her youth, she was so beautiful that her father Abu Sufyan used to say that there was no woman more beautiful than her in the whole of Arabia.[54]Umm Habiba, from her first husband had two children, a son and a daughter. Her daughter was brought up under the guardianship of the Prophet and was married to Daud bin Urwa, the richest man of the tribe of Saqeef.[55]

Umm Habiba was a staunch believer in Islam. She did not concede any point in respect of Islam to even her father. It is stated that once her father came to Madina to negotiate for the extension of the period of the treaty of Hudaybiyah but the Prophet did not agree to that. He also visited his daughter. When he went to her apartment and wanted to sit on the Prophet's bed, she rolled it up and told him not to sit on that. He asked his daughter "Am I too good for this bed or is it too good for me?" She replied that "It is the bed of the Messenger of Allah and you are an unclean idol worshipper".[56]

Once, the Prophet told her that the doors of Heaven would be opened for one who prays twelve *Nafil* prayers in a day. Since that day, she never missed her *Nafil* prayers.[57] On the death of her father; she discarded the customary lamentations after three days as per the saying of the Prophet.

Umm Habiba was a very devoted and courageous lady. During Khailafat of Uthman when the opponents had surrounded his house and he did not have anything to eat or drink, she took some eatables and water on a camel and proceeded towards his house. The opponents not only did not allow her to go but also misbehaved with her without making any concession for the Mother of Believers. With great difficulty she was rescued.[58]

She died at the age of seventy-two years. Before her death, she called Aisha and said, "There were some bad feelings between us. May Allah forgive me and you".There was sixty-five traditions ascribed to her in different books.

Safiyah Bint Hayayy Ibn Akhtab

1.	Parents name	Father: Huyayy bin Akhtab Mother: Barra bint Saurawal
2.	Age at the time of marriage	17 years
3.	Prophet's age at the time of marriage	57 years
4.	Marital status	Widow, twice married
5.	Children with the previous husbands	None
6.	Children with the prophet	None
7.	Age at the time of death	60 years
8.	Companionship with the Prophet	6 years
9.	Period of widowhood	37 years
10.	Number of traditions ascribed to her	10
11.	Buried at	Madina – Jannat ul Baqui

Safiyah's name was Zaynab, but the Prophet renamed her Safiyah. Her parents belonged to leading Jewish families. Her father Huyayy bin Akhtab, was the chief of Banu Nazeer tribe and traced its ancestry to the Prophet Haroon. Her mother Barra bint Saurawal also came from a very distinguished family of Quraiza. Safiyah was 17 years old at the time of her marriage with the Prophet.[59]

Safiyah was first married to Salm bin Mishkam Al Quraz, who was a poet and a warrior. Due to temperamental differences, the marriage was not successful and she was divorced. Then she was married to Kinanah ibn Abi Huqayq who was a very famous businessman.[60] They were married for only a month or two, before the Prophet set out to Madina.[61] Kinanah was not killed in the battle, but he was brought before the Prophet to find out the hidden treasure. He did not tell the truth and was killed.[62] It is not easy to believe that a girl of seventeen, whose father and husband were killed by the Muslims, had willingly accepted the new faith and preferred to marry the Prophet instead of joining her own people. This could be understood only if we look back at her background from her early childhood.

Safiyah, unlike her father and husband was of a deeply pious nature.

From her childhood, she had heard about the Prophet who was soon to come. People were talking of a person who claimed to be the Messenger of Allah and then came the news that he had come to Quba. She had also heard her father and uncle talking about the Prophet but while they believed the newcomer to be the promised Prophet, they still intended to oppose him.

Her young mind was puzzled from the very beginning on hearing such contradictory talks. Soon after her second marriage, she had a dream. She saw a brilliant moon hanging in the sky and she knew that beneath it laid the city of Madina. Then the moon began to move toward Khyber, where it fell into her lap. When she told her husband about the dream, he struck her on her face and said, "This can only mean that thou desired the King of Hijaz, Muhammad."[63] The mark on her face was still visible when she was brought to the Prophet and on his enquiry she told him of her dream.

The Jewish defeat in the Battle of Khyber was very devastating for them. It had crushed them completely. After the battle, all the prisoners were assembled and distributed among the victors. Safiyah was allotted to the Dihyah of the Banikab. There are different versions as how she came to the Prophet. According to one story, some people pointed out that since she was the daughter of the chief of the tribe, she deserved better treatment, so she should be taken to the Prophet. According to another version, Safiyah herself presented her case to the Prophet that she needed better treatment. A third version is that after hearing her plight, especially her dream, the Prophet decided to take her. It is believed that the Prophet gave Dihyah Kalb another girl and Safiyah came to the Prophet. He set her free and gave her the option either to go back to her people or accept Islam and marry him. She preferred the second option. When asked what dower he had given her, he replied that it was her freedom.

On his way to Madina, the Prophet halted at a place called Sahba, where he held the *Walima* feast. Abu Hurayra said that "When the Messenger of Allah, consummated the marriage, Abu Ayyub spent the night at the door of the Prophet. In the morning the Prophet said *takbir* and there was Abu Ayyub with his sword." He said "O Messenger of Allah. She is a girl who is new to Islam and marriage and you killed her father, brother and husband. I do not trust her with you." The Prophet laughed and spoke kindly to him to pacify his emotions.[64]

On her arrival at Madina, a large number of women came to see her. Though she was short statured, she was beautiful. The wives also came to see her although covered in veil. When Aisha was returning after seeing

Safiyah, the Prophet recognized her and asked her, "Aisha, how did you find her"? She said "She is Jewish". The Prophet remarked, "Don't say this. She has become a Muslim and her Islam is better"(Tabaqat).

Aisha's remark showed the jealously she had after seeing that beautiful lady. It was but natural for Aisha because every new wife was bound to snatch away from her the time and attention of the Prophet, of which once Aisha was the sole recipient.

In the beginning, Safiyah was not welcomed by the other wives. On many occasions, she was made to feel inferior because of her Jewish background. On one occasion, Aisha had passed remarks about her Jewish origin that were taken seriously by Safiyah, who wept and complained to the Prophet. The Prophet consoled her and said, "You should have told that your father was Haroon, Musa was your uncle and the husband is the holy Prophet of God".

It is related by Aisha that the Prophet was on a journey when Safiyah's camel fell sick. Zaynab bin Jahsh had some extra camels and the Prophet asked her to give one to Safiyah. Zaynab was known for her generosity, but on that occasion due to the jealousy among the wives, she said "I should give to that Jewess?" The Prophet felt bad and did not go to her quarter for two or three months.[65]

Before his death, when the Prophet was very ill, all his wives gathered around him. It is related that Safiyah said, "By Allah, O Messenger of Allah, I wish I was suffering instead of you". The wives of the Prophet winked at that and the Prophet looked at them and said, "Rinse out your mouths". They asked "for what?" The Prophet said, "You winked at her. By Allah, she spoke truthfully".[66] It is believed that she was deeply in love with the Prophet. Even when he was in *Itikaf* in the Mosque, she used to go and visit him often just to have a glimpse of him.

Safiyah was very sober by nature; she was dignified, patient and polite. She was a woman of very strong will and endurance. After the victory in the battle of Khyber, she was captured and was brought by Bilal before the Prophet, along with her cousin sister. She had to pass through heaps of dead bodies of the Jews, including the bodies of her father, brother and husband. Her cousin could not stand the sight and broke down and cried bitterly, but Safiyah calmly underwent this ordeal and did not show any sign of grief or mental suffering. When the Prophet came to know this he told Bilal that he should not have brought the ladies by that route.

Once Aisha remarked about her short stature on which the Prophet warned Aisha and said "Aisha you have told such a thing that if it was dropped in an ocean, it will spoil the water."

On his way to Madina, the Prophet got Safiyah mounted on his own camel and covered her with a robe, indicating that she had become his wife. After reaching Madina, she was lodged in one of the houses of his devoted and faithful companion, Haritha ibn Numan. Later on; an apartment was built for her along with the apartments of other wives.

Safiyah was a large hearted lady. Ibn Sa'd reports that she had only one residential house, which she had given in charity in her lifetime. She was also very sympathetic. It is reported that in the year 35 AH, rebels had stopped all supplies of food and water to Uthman and had besieged him in his house. She tried to take some food and water for him, but was obstructed and could not reach there. Then she deputed Hasan, the grandson of the Prophet to take the articles there.[67]

After the death of the Prophet, one of her servants once complained to Umar that she still cherishes Saturday - a good day for Jews - and relations with the Jews. Umar made enquiries from Safiyah. She said that she had no reason to cherish Saturday as God has given her Friday in place of Saturday. On her relations with the Jews, she remarked that they were her kith and kin and she had regard for her blood relations. Umar was pleased with her straightforwardness. She asked her servant what made her to complain to Umar and the servant said she was misled by the devil. Hearing that, she kept quiet and freed the slave girl.

Safiyah died in 50 AH at the age of 60. She was buried in Jannat-ul-Baqui. It is stated that she left 100,000 dirhams after the sale of her land and goods and she wanted one third of that to be given to her nephew, who was a Jew.There was opposition to this but Aisha warned them of her will.[68]

She was the storehouse of knowledge. She used to have huge gatherings of women at her place, trying to resolve their queries about Islam. Ten traditions have been ascribed to her.

Maymunah Bint Haris

1.	Parents name	Father: Haris bin Hazan Mother: Hind bint Zaher
2.	Age at the time of marriage	36 or 50 years – Difference of opinion
3.	Prophet's age at the time of marriage	59 years
4.	Marital status	Widow, twice married
5.	Children with the previous husbands	None
6.	Children with the prophet	None
7.	Age at the time of death	80 years
8.	Companionship with the Prophet	4 years
9.	Period of widowhood	NA
10.	Number of traditions ascribed to her	76
11.	Buried at	Sarif

Maymunah's original name was Burrah. After the marriage, the Prophet gave her the name Maymunah. Her father was Haris bin Hazan, who belonged to the tribe of Quraish. Her mother was Hind bint Zaher. Maymunah was the sister of Umm Fazal, the wife of Abbas who was the Prophet's uncle. Maymunah was twice married. Her first husband was Masud bin Amr. After the divorce, she was married to Abu Rahm bin Abdul Uzza, who died in 7 AH. She was an elderly lady and had suffered a lot in life. Abbas, the uncle of the Prophet, initiated the marriage proposal[69] on the suggestion of his wife.

It is believed that Maymunah yearned to marry the Prophet. She went to her sister and talked to her about her desire, which in turn talked to her husband, Abbas. The Prophet accepted the proposal, since it was bound to improve relationship between the Prophet and the influential people of Mecca. It is said that when this good news reached her she was on a camel. She immediately got off the camel and said, "What is on it is for the Messenger of Allah". The marriage took place in the background of the treaty of Hudaybiyah according to which the Prophet along with his fellow men was permitted to go to Mecca and stay there for three days to perform Umrah. It was at this time, when the Prophet was in *Ihram* that the proposal for marriage came.

When the three days were over, the Quraish asked them to go back. The marriage was not solemnized. The Prophet and his fellow men wanted to extend the stay for one more day to have the *walima* feast there, but the Quraish did not agree to their request. The Prophet did not like to have any ill feelings so they marched towards Madina and after going about ten miles, halted at a place called Sarif. The Prophet offered 400 dirhams as dower to her. This was the last marriage of the Prophet, as he did not marry after that. It is believed that verse of *banning* was revealed at that time:

It shall be unlawful for you O Muhammad; to marry more women after this or to change your present wives with other women.
Al Ahzab: 33: 52

Maymunah was an elderly lady but there is a difference of opinion about her age. Some have mentioned that she was about fifty years old while some others believed that she was in her thirties[70]. She died at the age of 80. As per her will, she was buried in Sarif, where her marriage with the Prophet was performed.

This marriage proved fruitful for the mission of Islam as many individuals and parties came into the fold of Islam after this marriage. Most important among them was Khalid bin Walid, the great warrier, who was Maymunah's nephew. After the marriage, he along with large number of his followers embraced Islam.[71]

Maymunah was a woman of simple living and high thinking. She used to wear very ordinary clothes. After the Prophet's death she used to shave her head. She was very God fearing and had great regard for the rights of her kith and kin. She was fond of freeing slaves. She used to borrow money. Once, she borrowed a large sum of money and some one asked her how she was going to pay it back. She said God helps those who have the intention to pay back the amount. The Prophet called her a symbol of goodness.

Conclusion

The above description of the wives of the Prophet and a glance at the women companions of the Prophet shows that women were active in every sphere of life. There was no field, which was out of their reach. They participated in every sphere of life. They were active in educational, religious, political, commercial and even in battlefields. In the battlefield, the wives of the Prophet such as Aisha and Umm Salamah had helped not only in providing water to the wounded soldiers but also in nursing the wounded and giving firstaid to them. In the religious field, they had a very impressive role to play. They spread the message of the new religion and brought into the fold of Islam, many men and women. They led the women in prayers.

There are many things, which girls of today can learn from the lives of these eminent ladies, for example, their simplicity, modesty, devotion, patience and cordial relations with their husbands and co-wives. These are some of the virtues that gave these women a special position and status in history. These qualities are gradually diminishing from women of the present generation, giving rise to social disruptions. It is time to look back and make a realistic assessment of the situation so as to make this life and the life in the hereafter a fruitful one.

References and Notes

1. Martin Lings, op. cit. p. 34.
2. Ibid. p. 35.
3. Abbasi Madani, op. cit.p. 89.
4. A musical instrument generally played in marriages.
5. Adil Salahi: Muhammad, Man and Prophet, 1995, p. 73.
6. Maudoodi: Sirat Sarwar –e- Alam, quoted by Afrog Hasan, Azwaj Mutharhat, vol.1.p. 115.
7. Mubarkpuri, op. cit. p. 125.
8. Ali Asghar, op. cit. p. 84, Ibn Sa'd, op. cit. p. 42.
9. Tabaqat, quoted by Ibn Sa'd, op. cit., p 101.
10. Ali Asghar, op. cit. p. 84.
11. Muslim, Bukhari, Sulaman Nadvi, Martin Lings, , Mubarkpuri, Abbasi Madani and Afrog Hasan, all have agreed that Aisha was 6 or 7 years old at the time of marriage and 9 or 10, when she joined the Prophet at Madina.
12. Martin Lings, op. cit. p. 106. Also narrated by Bukhari and others on Sunnah.
13. Afrog Hasan, op. cit. Vol. I, 1996, p. 187.
14. Martin Lings, op. cit. p. 133.
15. Abbasi Madani, op. cit. p. 106.
16. Sulaman Nadvi: Sirat – e – Aisha, Mushtaq Book Corner, Lahore, p. 30.
17. There are two versions about the necklace. As per the first version, the necklace belonged to Aisha's sister (Ali Ashgar Chowdhri: op. cit. p. 94.) As per the second version, Aisha's mother had given this necklace to her at the time of marriage (Martin Lings, op. cit. p. 240.)
18. Martin Lings, op. cit.p. 240.
19. Ibid. p 241.
20. Ibid. p. 245.
21. Zakaria Bashier: Sunshine at Madina, op. cit. p. 150.
22. Martin Lings, op. cit., p. 315.
23. Red faced lady-Zakaria Bashier: Sunshine at Madina, op. cit., p.
24. 149.

25. Ibid., p. 149, p. 150.
26. Sulaman Nadvi, op. cit., p. 47.
27. Martin Lings, op. cit., p. 164,
28. Zakaria Bahier: Sunshine at Madina, op. cit., p. 144.
29. Abbasi Madani, op. cit., p. 133.
30. Ibid.
31. There is a difference of opinion some writers have mentioned that she was divorsed.
32. Zakaria Bahsier: Sunshine at Madina, op. cit., p. 149
33. Abbasi Madani op. cit.,, p. 137
34. Ali Asghar. Op. cit. p. 149.
35. Ibid.
36. 34.Martin Lings, op. cit., p. 206.
37. Ali Asghar. Op.cit.p 160.
38. Ibid.
39. Ibid., p. 207.
40. Ali Asghar, op. cit., p. 235.
41. Ibid., p. 235
42. Mubarakpuri, op. cit., p. 344.
43. Umm Ayman was older to Zayad at least by twenty years.
44. Afrog Hasan, Vol. II, op. cit., p. 56.
45. Ibid., p. 54.
46. Abbasi Madani, op. cit, p. 159.
47. Ibid., p. 158.
48. Afrog Hasan, Vol. II, op. cit., p. 101.
49. Martin Lings, op. cit., p. 242.
50. Asghar Ali, op. cit., p.197.
51. Martin Lings, op. cit., pp. 241, 242.
52. Ibid.
53. Ibid., p. 259.
54. Abbasi Madani, op. cit., p. 165.
55. Ibid., p. 164.
56. Ibid. ., p. 166
57. Ibid, p. 166.
58. Ibid. p.167
59. Martin Lings. Op. cit. p. 268
60. Asghar Ali, op. cit., p. 207, Abbasi Madani op. cit., p. 167.
61. Martin Lings, op. cit., p. 268.
62. Ibid. .,

63. Ibid.
64. Ibid p. 268.
65. Ibid, p. 90.
66. Ibid.
67. Afrog Hasan op. cit. p. 186
68. Ibid p. 196
69. Abbasi Madani op. cit. p. 173.
70. Ibid. p. 174. p. 171.
71. Ibid. p.175.
72. Ibn Sa'd op.cit.p. 91.
73. Abbasi Madani. Says she was 51 years old (p. 176) where as Asghar Ali mentions that she was 38 years old.(p. 228)
74. Abbasi Madani. Op. cit p. 171.

Slave girls

The critics of the Prophet had also pointed out the presence of slave girls like Rehana and Maria. But this cannot be attributed to sexual desire, as at that time he already had a number of wives. This has to be understood in the proper social context. Islam is the religion which belives in equality and equal treatment to all human beings. The Prophet Muhammad(S) condemned slavery and encouraged people to free slaves. He realized that slavery could not be eradicated over night since it is as old as the concept of war itself. His many companions like Abu Bakr and Umar, were in the habit of freeing slaves.

Secondly the wars had created the problem of prisoners. They had to be given humane treatment. They had to be provided with proper food, clothing and sheltre. This was not possible because they had neither institutional arrangement nor they had the means to do that, and hence it was considered desirable to distribute the prisoners of war among the warriors so that they could take care of them.

Among the prisoners, there were women also, who were distributed among the soldiers as bounty. The soldier to which a woman was allotted only had the right over her, and not any other person, and if she gave birth to a child it was known as his child. Hager, the slave woman of Prophet Ibrahim gave birth to Ismail, Maria gave birth to Ibrahim, who was known as the Prophet's son.

If we compare past with the present situation, we are shocked to see the picture of war crimes against women.

The Prophet in view of the social status of some of the women prisoners such as Juwayriah and Safiyah, who were daughters of chief of the tribes, took them as his wives. Though after embrassing Islam he wanted to extend the same facility to the slave girl Rehana as well but she was not willing. By the time Maria was brought to him it is believed the Ayaha putting a ban on further wives was already revealed, and hence she could not get the status of a wife.

a) *Rehana*

The conquest of Bani Qurayzab gave a good bounty to Muslims. Among other things, there were a number of slaves, one of them was Rehana. She was the daughter of Zayda Nadirite. She was married to a man of Qurayzah.[1] She came as a slave and remained as such until her death. She died five years after the death of the Prophet.

Rehana was also very beautiful and attractive. At first the Prophet had put her in the care of his aunt Salma in whose house Rafiah had already taken refuge. In the beginning she did not like to embrace Islam, but later on she entered into the new faith. When Rafiah gave the happy news to the Prophet, the Prophet offered to free her and make her his wife, but she preferred to maintain the status quo. She said "O messenger of God, leave me in thy power that will be easier for me and for thee."[2]

Some writers have made a mention of Rehana but they have not been able to depict a clear picture of her status. Many of them are silent on this issue but as is evident from the historical fact, she was merely a slave girl.

b) *Maria Qibtia*

After establishing the Islamic State in Madina, the Prophet concentrated his efforts in extending the boundaries of Islam. With this objective in mind, after the treaty of Hudaibiyah, he wrote letters and sent emissaries to a number of Kings and Chiefs, extending them the invitation to accept Islam. While the response of some of them was positive, the others were negative and indifferent.

The Prophet had sent a letter to the Egyptian Chief for the same purpose. The Chief was very cordial and warm in his response. Although he did not accept Islam, he sent a number of gifts to the Prophet. Along with the gifts, there were two very beautiful Coptic slave girls, Maria and her sister Sirin. The King mentioned that they belonged to a respectable family and deserved better treatment. Of the two, Maria was extremely beautiful. The Prophet kept her for himself and gave Sirin to Hassan ibn Thabil.[3] It is believed that the two girls had already embraced Islam before they reached Madina.[4]

Aisha has narrated, "I was not jealous of any woman except for my jealousy towards Maria. That was because she was beautiful. The Messenger of Allah admired her when she was first brought to him. He put her in the house of Haritha ibn Numan. She was our neighbor. Then he moved her to Al-Aliyya".[5]

Maria gave birth to a son and Gabriel came and addressed the Prophet as 'father of Ibrahim'. Salama, an elderly woman, who had attended all deliveries of Khadijah, also took care of the birth of this child. The child was born at night and the next morning after the dawn prayer, the Prophet gave the good news to his companions. There was great rejoicing in Madina and great rivalry among the women as to who should be the foster mother. The choice fell on the wife of a blacksmith in upper Madina, near the house of Maria.

The Prophet was naturally very happy at the birth of his son. He used to visit him every day, but his happiness was short lived. Ibrahim fell sick and there was no hope of his survival. Maria and her sister were attending to him all the time. Even the Prophet used to visit him and was with him at the time of his death. He took the child in his hands and tears rolled down from his cheeks. He became extremely emotional and disturbed. His companion, H. Abdur Rahman, remarked "O Prophet of Allah, you have prohibited Muslims from shedding tears in this way, if they see you weeping; they will lose control and will start weeping."

The Prophet replied "It is only the feeling of pity and one who has no pity for others does not get pity.[6] I have prohibited people from lamentation". The Prophet led the funeral prayers. He was buried in the graveyard of Jannat-ul-Baqui. Maria died five years after her son's death. She was also buried in the same graveyard.

Maria's status in the household is a controversial issue. The question is, was she a wife or merely a slave girl? Opinion is divided on this issue. While most of the writers have mentioned that the Prophet had eleven wives, which of course does not include Maria, there are some who have mentioned that he had twelve or even thirteen wives. I understand that Maria was merely a slave girl.

The Prophet had allotted turns to his wives and he was very particular to follow that till his death, but in case of Maria there was no such restriction and as reported, he used to visit her very often. After the Prophet's marriage with Maymunah, his last wife, the Revelation came prohibiting him from further marriages. Maria came as a slave to him after that Revelation and hence her inclusion among the wives does not arise. Some people consider her as Prophet's wife just because she was the mother of his son Ibrahim.

References & Notes

1. Martin Lings, op.cit. p. 233.
2. Ibid.
3. Martin Lings, op. cit. p. 277
4. Abbasi Madani.,op. cit. p. 183.
5. Ibn Sa'd, op. cit. p. 149.
6. Abbasi Madani, op. cit. p. 220.

Part IV

Children and Grand Children
Of The Prophet

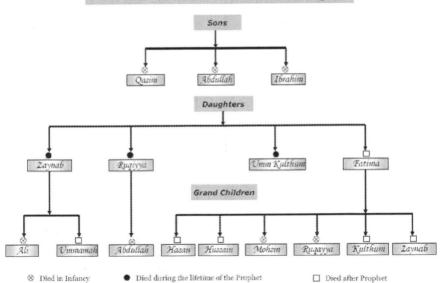

Children and Grand Children of the Prophet

Sons

Qasim | Abdullah | Ibrahim

Daughters

Zaynab | Ruqiyya | Umm Kulthum | Fatima

Grand Children

Ali | Ummamah | Abdullah | Hasan | Hussain | Mohsin | Ruqayya | Kulthum | Zaynab

⊗ Died in Infancy ● Died during the lifetime of the Prophet ☐ Died after Prophet

Son-in-Laws

Sl.No.	Name	Wive's Name
1	Abu al–Aas	Zaynab
2	Uthaman ibn Affan	1. Ruqiyya 2. Umm Kulthum
3	Ali ibn Abu Talib	Fatima

Prophet Muhammad(S) greatly loved children. It is generally agreed that he had six children from his first wife Khadijah and one son from Maria, the Coptic slave girl. Exact details about the children are not available in an authentic way. The reason for this is that all his children, except the last son Ibrahim, were born before Prophethood, when history was not recorded in its proper form, nor did he have his devoted group of companions who would have remembered the details. Secondly, some of the facts have been deliberately distorted due to religious conflicts.

An unbiased view reveals that he had two sons and four daughters from his first wife Khadijah and in his old age he had another son from Maria, but none of the three sons survived and all of them died in their infancy. All the four girls survived, got married and had children. While three of them died during the lifetime of the Prophet, only the youngest one, Fatima, survived after his death.

Although there is some difference of opinion on the sequence of the birth of his children, there is general agreement on the following order:

1. Qasim was his first child and his eldest son.
2. Zaynab, the second child and the eldest daughter.
3. Abdullah, the second son.
4. Ruqayya, the second daughter
5. Umm Kulthum, the third daughter
6. Fatima, the fourth and the youngest daughter.
7. Ibrahim, the youngst son.

In the Arab society of that time, great importance was attached to sons, and the birth of daughter was not welcomed in the family to the extent that many newborn girls were buried alive. Secondly, it was generally presumed that the family lineage was only through the sons and not through the daughters, but in the case of the Prophet; it was through his daughter Fatima's sons Hasan and Hussain.

God enhanced the positions of girls by giving four daughters to the Prophet. The way the Prophet loved his daughters removed all differences between sons and daughters and an effort was made to see that the daughters were not considered to be a burden on the family. In spite of the progress of society, the position of girls has not improved to the extent desirable and girls still have a secondary position in most families.

Son's Of The Prophet

Qasim

The first child born to the Prophet was his son Qasim. Although the exact date of birth is not available, it is believed that he was born ten or eleven years before Prophethood. The Prophet kept his "kunniyat" (name by association to the progeny) as Abul Qasim.[1] Naturally, the parents were most happy, but their happiness was short-lived as the child died at an early age. Although the exact age could not be determined, it is believed that he was less than two years old. The reason for his death is also not known.

Abdullah

After Qasim, Abdullah was born, but he too died in infancy. There was some confusion about his name, as he was also called Tayab and Tahir. Some writers have mentioned that they were different children, but research reveals that it was Abdullah who was called by these names.

The death of Abdullah was a great blow to the Prophet as he was already under great stress due to severe opposition by his enemies. This provided another opportunity to his opponents to humiliate him. Instead of sympathizing with him, they were very jubilant as they thought that there would be no one to take his name in future, as it was generally believed that the son carried the family lineage. The Quraish used to say that the Prophet was helpless and had been cut off from the community. He was like a tree, which had been cut down to its roots (Abtar).

When Abdullah died, the Prophet's uncle Abu Lahab, who used to live on the opposite side of the Prophet's house, went running to the infidels and opponents of the Prophet telling them gleefully "tonight Muhammad had become like a tree without roots". It was in this background that Surah

Al-Kausar was revealed, which gave the good news that the Prophet had everything in abundance and it will be his opponents who will be cut off from their roots.

> *O Muhammad, surely we have granted you the Kauthar*
> *(Countless blessings – it is also the name of a special fountain*
> *which will be granted to the Prophet on the Day of Judgment),*
> *therefore offer Salah to your Lord and sacrifice. Surely,*
> *your enemy is the one who will be cut off from the roots*
> *Al – Kausar: 108:1-3*

Ibrahim

Although the Prophet had four daughters and he loved them very much, it was but natural for him to desire to have a son also. When Gabriel gave him the good news that he would be the father of Ibrahim, the Prophet was extremely happy. Ibrahim was born on 8th Zil Hajh in 8 AH from Maria. When Ibrahim was born, except Fatima, all other girls had died. The Prophet could have never imagined that his happiness would be short lived this time too.

Ibrahim was very fair and plump. On the 7th day, the Prophet performed his *Aqeeqa* (shaving of hair) by sacrificing a goat and also gave the silver equivalent of his hair in weight. There was great competition among women to be his wet nurse. Ultimately, the choice fell on a blacksmith woman who used to stay in the locality of Banu Najjar, in the neighborhood of Madina. The Prophet used to visit the house generally during noon and had his siesta there.

When Ibrahim was about sixteen months old, he fell sick and died. This was of course a great shock to the Prophet. He submitted to the will of God.He could not control his grief and tears rolled down his cheeks, When Ibrahim died, there was a solar eclipse too, people attributed his death to it as it was considered to be an inauspicious day, but the Prophet refuted this notion.[2]

Daughters Of The Prophet

Zaynab

She was the eldest daughter of the Prophet. Some writers are of the opinion that she was the eldest child, while some others believe that Qasim was the eldest. She was born ten years before Prophethood, when the Prophet was thirty-five years old.

Zaynab was married to her cousin (aunt's son) Abu al-Aas. [3] He was a very noble person. He loved Zaynab very much. Zaynab embraced Islam in her childhood, but her husband remained a non-believer for a long time. Zaynab was living happily with him because till that time the verse prohibiting the marriage of a believer with a non-believer had not been revealed.

Three years after Prophethood, when the Prophet came out openly to defend his new faith, there was naturally a lot of opposition. His own relatives were not convinced and they wanted him to give up the advocacy of the new religion. When, in order to deter him, his uncle Abu Lahab asked his two sons to divorce the two daughters of the Prophet, Ruqayya and Umm Kulthum, [4] some people approached Abu al-Aas to take the similar step towards Zaynab. Great pressure was put on him. They went to the extent of suggesting that he should look for the richest and most beautiful bride in Mecca, but Abu al-Aas was deeply in love with Zaynab, he bluntly refused. Zaynab always hoped and prayed that her husband would embrace Islam.

In the thirteenth year of Prophethood, the Prophet migrated to Madina, and later on his two daughters, Umm Kulthum and Fatima joined him, but Zaynab remained with her husband in Mecca. In the battle of Badr, Abu al-Aas fought against the Muslims. When the Muslims won the battle, he became a prisoner. When the people of Mecca ransomed their captives, his brother Amr bin Ar Rabi came to give ransom for his brother. Zaynab had sent her onyx necklace as part of her husband's ransom.[5] When the Prophet saw the necklace he became emotional because that necklace belonged to his beloved wife Khadijah who had given it to her daughter at the time of her marriage. He said to his companions, "If you can see a way to release the captive and return the goods to him, do it".[6] His companions readily agreed to do so. It is narrated that before he left, the Prophet spoke to Abu al-Aas. It is believed that he asked him to send Zaynab to him, as by that time the Revelation had made it clear that a Muslim woman could not be the wife of a non–believer. Abu al-Aas agreed to this condition with a heavy heart, but even after his return to Mecca, he did not embrace Islam and that was a point of great distress to the Prophet who did not want to separate a wife from her husband but was forced to do it by the will of God.

After coming to Mecca, Abul al-Aas made all the preparations to send Zaynab to Madina. His brother Kinanab was to escort her. The arrangements were made in secret, but they started for Madina in daylight. This was noticed by the non–believers and some of them started following them in order to stop them for proceeding towards Madina. When some people came close to Zaynab, she was pushed and fell down from the camel. She was pregnant and started bleeding.

This outraged Kinanab who took out an arrow and challenged the intercepters. Realizing that the situation was going out of control, the leader of the gang Abu Sufyan came forward to talk to Kinanab. He explained to him that they had no objection to Zaynab's going to Madina but as they were already humiliated by the Muslims, this step would add insult to injury so he advised him to take Zaynab after some time and in darkness to avoid further humiliation.[7] Kinanab agreed and Zaynab joined the Prophet in Madina after a few days.

About five months after the campaign of the Trench, the Prophet got the news that a rich Caravan of the Quraish was on its way from Syria. Zayd, with a troop of a hundred and seventy horses, was sent to waylay it. The entire merchandise was captured and the men were taken captive, but some of them escaped. Abu al-Aas was one of them. When he was passing through the vicinity of Madina, he had the desire to see his wife Zaynab and the little daughter Ummamah. In the darkness he managed to reach them and Zaynab gave him protection. At dawn, she went to the Mosque as usual. Before the prayer started, she cried out loudly "O people, I gave protection to Abu al-Abu al-Aas".

When the prayer was over, the Prophet addressed the gathering and said, "Did you hear what I heard"? Then he said, "I know naught of this until I hear what you heard. The meanest Muslim can grant protection, which shall be binding on all other Muslims."[8] Then he went to his daughter and said "Receive him with all honor, but let him not come unto thee as a husband, for thou are not his by law."

Zaynab pleaded with her father to return his merchandise, as that belonged to different people of the Quraish who had trusted him. The Prophet sent word to the people requesting them if they could return the merchandise, he would be pleased, but if they didn't, they had a right over it. The people agreed to return everything as they valued the sentiments of the Prophet. Abu al-Aas went back to Mecca and returned the goods to the people. Then he came back to Madina and embraced Islam and was married to Zaynab as per the Islamic laws. However, the couple could hardly stay together for a year, as Zaynab died in 8 AH due to her sickness

The Prophet loved his daughter very much. He was naturally aggrieved over her death and used to say that Zaynab suffered because of him. The Prophet was with Zaynab till the end. After they gave her a bath, he took off an undergarment he was wearing and told them to wrap her in it before they shrouded her. Then he led the funeral prayer.

Zaynab had a son and a daughter. As per reliable sources, her son died in his infancy. Her daughter Ummamah, after the death of Fatima, was married to Ali the fourth Caliph. When Ali was on his deathbed, he made a will that Mughirah should marry her after his death. Mughirah married her, but some reports deny it.

Ruqayya

She was the second daughter of the Prophet. She was born seven years before Prophethood, when the Prophet was about thirty-three years old. It is believed that she was extremely beautiful. She had a very attractive figure and people used to admire her beauty Ruqayya was first married to Utbah–bin Abu Lahab, but their marriage was not consummated and she was living with her father. In the early days of Prophethood, the Prophet suffered great opposition from all corners, including his own close relatives. One of the staunch opponents was the Prophet's own uncle Abu Lahab. When the verse "Perish the hands of Abu Lahab" was revealed, Abu Lahab became wild and ordered his sons to divorce the daughters of Muhammad.

This proved to be a blessing in disguise, as Ruqayya got a very noble and handsome husband, Uthman bin Affan. It is narrated that Uthman had a desire to marry Ruqayya but before he could ask for her hand, he came to know that she was married to Utbah. One day, his aunt S'oda came. She was a good fortuneteller. She praised Prophet Muhammad(S) and gave a hint that Uthman would be marrying his daughter. Uthman was a wealthy, handsome and noble person, but he was a non-believer. After a few days, he went to Abu Bakr who also advised him to see Muhammad. Uthman went to the Prophet and the Prophet said "O Uthman, Almighty Allah invites you to Paradise, you must accept this call." Uthman was very much impressed by the talk of the Prophet and he immediately recited the *Kalimah* and embraced Islam. He was married to Ruqayya. She was not only the most beautiful of all the daughters, but perhaps the most beautiful woman of her generation in Mecca. Similarly, Uthman was also an extremely handsome man. To see both of them together was in itself a reason for rejoicing. In the 5th year of Prophethood, Uthman, along with his wife Ruqayya, migrated to Abyssinia. For the first time, the Prophet remarked that after Lot and Abraham, Uthman was the first person to migrate with his wife. After some time, both of them came back to Mecca presuming that the conditions in Mecca had become normal, but when they came to know that things had gone from bad to worse, they went back to Abyssinia again. The Prophet was worried, as he did not get any news from them for quite some time. Then one day, a woman came to the Prophet and told him that she had seen them in good health. The Prophet remarked, "Allah may be merciful towards them Uthman is the first person who had migrated with his family."

After a long stay, they came back to Mecca for a short period and then migrated to Madina where the Prophet had already migrated with his other two daughters. Just before the battle of Badr, Ruqayya had an attack of small pox. As the Prophet had to go, he asked Uthman to look after her but she could not recover from her illness and died in the month of Ramadan in 2 AH. When Ruqayya was being laid down in the grave, Zayd entered the city with the news of victory.[9]

After coming to Madina, he first went to Ruqayyah's grave with Fatima. Fatima was greatly distressed by the loss of her sister. Tears poured down from her cheeks. This was the first death in the family after the death of Khadijah. The Prophet had earlier spoken against lamentations for the dead, but this had led to a misunderstanding. When the Prophet returned from the cemetery, he heard the voice of Umar in anger against the women who were weeping for the martyrs of Badr and for Ruqayya. The Prophet said, "Umar, let them weep, what cometh from the heart and from the eye that is from God and His Mercy, but what cometh from the hand and from the tongue that is from Satan". By the hand, he meant the beating of the breast and the lacerating of the cheeks.[10] Ruqayya had given birth to a son named Abdullah, who died at the age of six.

Umm Kulthum

Umm Kulthum was the third daughter of the Prophet. She was born six years before Prophethood. She was one year younger to Ruqayya. Like Ruqayya, she was also married in childhood to Utaiba, the son of Abu Lahab and got divorced after the Revelation of the verses about Abu Lahab. She migrated to Madina along with her sister Fatima.

After the death of Ruqayya, Umar approached Uthman with the proposal that he marry his daughter Hafsah, but Uthman was not in a mood to get married since he used to be very depressed those days. Once, the Prophet asked him the reason for his sadness and he said that it was due to the death of Ruqayya that has disrupted his relationship with the Prophet. As they were talking, the Prophet said to Uthman "O Uthman, Gabriel has come and given the good news that I should give you my daughter Umm Kulthum in marriage." [11] Umm Kulthum was married to Uthman in Rabi ul Awal in 3 AH. She died six years after the marriage in Shaban in 9 AH. The Prophet led her funeral prayer. The Prophet had great regard for Uthman. He said that if he had one more daughter, he would have married her to Uthman. In one Hadis, it was mentioned that the Prophet said that if he had forty daughters, he would have married them to Uthman, one after the other. This only shows the great love and regard he had for Uthman.

The Prophet was greatly saddened by Umm Kulthum's death. Umm Kulthum did not have any child.

Fatima

Fatima was the youngest daughter of the Prophet and she was the only one who had survived after the death of the Prophet. It is believed that she was born five years before the Prophthood when the Prophet was thirty five years old and Khadijah was fifty years old. It is said that she was born when the Kabah was under construction.

From her childhood, Fatima wasn't like other girls who were fond of playing. For instance, Aisha used to play with her dolls along with her friends even after marriage, but Fatima never liked these things. She was very sober and used to keep herself aloof. It is said that she was more like her father. Aisha had remarked that after the death of Khadijah, even though Fatima was very young, she used to take care of her father. It is narrated that once when the Prophet was praying in the Kabah, in order to humiliate him, one person by name Uqbah Abi Mu'ayt went to the extent that he brought the entrails of a camel and flung them on the Prophet's neck when he was prostrating. He could not even lift his head[12] someone went and reported this to Fatima who came running and removed the unclean stuff cursed the evildoers and prayed that God punish them. Many a time she used to clean his head, which used to be full of saw dust thrown on him by his enemies Fatima used to have tears in her eyes, on such occasions but the Prophet always consoled her.

The Prophet received many proposals for Fatima's marriage. Abu Bakr and Umar both approached him, but he ignored them. Then it is believed that they asked Ali to ask for Fatima's hand. The Prophet had brought up Ali and he was living with them. He had a liking for Fatima but was hesitating because of his poverty. As most of the time he was with the Prophet, he could not take up any job; hence he had no means of livelihood. On the advice of his friends, he approached the Prophet. The Prophet, in his turn had already decided to marry Fatima to him but he asked Ali if he had anything to give in dower. Ali said that he had nothing. The Prophet then reminded him that he had armour, which he had given to him after the battle of Badr. [13] It is believed that he sold this for 480 dirhams and used it towards his marriage.

There is another story that Ali had two camels that he wanted to sell so that he could use that amount for his marriage. One day, when he came back, he found that his uncle Hamza, who was drunk, (drinking was not prohibited then) had slaughtered them in order to make a feast out of them. Ali, on seeing this was badly upset. When Uthman saw him in this condition, he asked him what was wrong. When Ali told him that he had no money for his marriage, Uthman said, "Do not worry; spend as much as you want, I will take care of the expenses". This showed how generous Uthman was.

There is a difference of opinion about the age of Fatima at the time of marriage. Some have mentioned that she was about fifteen years old and Ali was twenty one while some other writers have mentioned that she was twenty. It is believed that the marriage took place in the month of Moharram of 2 AH perhaps a few months after Aisha came to live with the Prophet in Madina. Aisha has given a detailed account of the preparations made for Fatima's marriage. She has stated that Umm Salamah went with Aisha to make the house ready for the bridal couple and to prepare food. She stated that soft sand was brought from the riverbed and scattered over the earthen floor of the house. The bridal bed was a sheepskin and there was a faded cover of striped cloth from Yemen. For a pillow, they stuffed a leather cushion with palm fiber. Then they laid out dates and figs for the guests to eat in addition to the main meal and filled the water skin with water they had perfumed. It was generally agreed that this wedding feast was one of the finest in Madina at that time. After the *Nikah* (wed lock) there was a *Walima* feast the next day. One of his companions, by the name of Sa'd, offered a goat and the Ansar tribe contributed towards other expenses. It was said to be one of the best *Walima* dinner.

One can have an idea of how simple the marriage was by having a look at the list of items, which the Prophet gave to his beloved daughter by way of dowry, and compare it with the custom these days. The items, which were given to Fatima, were: [14]

1. A carved wooden bed
2. A mattress stuffed with wool
3. A leather pillow stuffed with the bark of date trees
4. One leather skin to carry water
5. One cup
6. Two grinding stones
7. Two earthen pots
8. Two bed sheets and
9. One prayer rug

During the Prophet's time, there was no tradition of giving dowry, from the side of the bride. Nor did the Prophet give these things to his other daughters. It was the responsibility of the bridegroom to provide the basic things to his wife as the Prophet used to do for his wives. However, in the case of Fatima, he had to do this as he had brought up Ali who had no income of his own. Today, the picture is altogether different. It is the bride's side that is supposed to provide everything.

The Prophet told Fatima, "By Allah, I swear that I have married you to the best of my family". Ali had taken a house near the Prophet's house, but this was at a distance. The Prophet used to go daily to see her. He expressed a desire to get her close to his own house. Haris bin Nawman had a number of houses near the Mosque and quite a few had already been given to the Prophet's wives. When he came to know of the Prophet's desire, he immediately vacated one near the Prophet's house to accommodate them.

Fatima and Ali had a peaceful married life. Whenever there was any friction between the two, the Prophet used to go to their house and smooth out the wrinkles. Fatima and Ali were both very hard working. They had to do all the household work. Ali used to do the outside work; even cutting the wood, while Fatima did all the inside work. In those days, there were no facilities like what we have to day. Even the grinding of grain to make flour was done by hand. Fatima had to do the cooking, washing, cleaning and looking after the children all by herself. In the Prophet's house, there were some devoted people like Umm Ayman, Anas, Abu Rafi and others who used to share the work, but here the entire burden was on her. Moreover, Ali had hardly any income. This added to their difficulties and had an adverse effect on Fatima's health.

It is believed that once the Prophet got a few slaves by way of bounty. When Ali came to know, he asked Fatima to go and ask him to spare one servant for her. When Fatima approached him, the Prophet bluntly refused on the ground that there are people who are more in need of money. He told Fatima that he could suggest an alternative, which would give her strength to do her work. Then he advised her to recite every night *"Subhan Allah"* thirty three times, *"Alhamdu Lillah"* thirty three times and *"Allah ho Akbar"*, thirty four times. This is known as Tasbeeh–e– Fatima.This shows that in spite of the fact that the Prophet loved his daughter, he could not oblige her in preference to other members of the community.

Various incidents of that time showed that the economy was in a bad shape. The Prophet himself was undergoing such hardship that for days together he did not have anything to eat. Once, when he went to Fatima's house, she told the Prophet that she and her children were hungry and had nothing to eat. The Prophet told her "My daughter, I am also hungry for the past three days. If I had prayed to God He would have granted me what I wanted, but I prefer the other world to this world. You, my daughter, do not lose patience. You are the leader of the women of paradise."[15]

Once, she had baked some bread for her children and brought a piece for her father. The Prophet said "I have not eaten anything for the past three days." Once, the Prophet was hungry and there was nothing in

Fatima's house also. When he went out, he met Abu Bakr and Umar who were also hungry. All of them went to Abu Ayyub Ansari who was in his garden at that time. He immediately slaughtered a goat and prepared food for them. The Prophet kept some meat on bread and asked him to send it to Fatima who was also hungry for the past many days.

There are many traditions, which show that most of the time they had nothing to eat, but they never complained. Fatima was all the time busy in prayers. Even while doing household work like grinding flour, instead of singing songs; she used to recite the Quran. It is a good example to follow, as most of us complain about lack of time for our prayers while working in the house or traveling. Now a days, as most people have to drive long distances, we can follow this example.

The Prophet loved Fatima so much that whenever she used to come to him, he used to get up and kiss her on the forehead. It was his practice that whenever he used to go out of Madina, the last person he used to visit was Fatima, and on his return, he used to go to her first.

Once, Abu Jahl's brother, who was a bitter enemy of the Prophet, suggested to Ali that he should marry Ghora bint Abu Jahal. Ali agreed to this suggestion, as it was common among Arab to have more than one wife. However, when the Prophet came to know, he was very upset and expressed his disapproval openly "The house of Hisham (Abu Jahl's family), seeks my permission to marry their daughter to Ali, but I will not permit this. I will never allow this. However, the son of Abu Talib may divorce my daughter and may marry their daughter. Fatima is a part of my body and he who torments her will hurt me."

"Anybody harming her will harm me." He further added "I do not want to convert lawful into unlawful and unlawful into lawful. But by Allah, the daughter of the Messenger of Allah and the daughter of the enemy of Allah cannot be together."[16] Ali gave up the idea of having a second wife in the lifetime of Fatima. He married Ummamah, Zaynab's daughter after the death of Fatima and had more wives after that.

When the Prophet died, Fatima was near his bed. Before his death, he whispered something in her ear, which made her weep, and then again he whispered something that made her smile. When Aisha asked her what made her weep and then why was she smiling, she told her the secret that the Prophet first whispered in her ears that the Angel Gabriel used to recite the Quran once a year, but this year he recited the Quran twice and from this he inferred that his end was near. This made me weep. Then he said that she would be the first to join him and she would be the leader of the women of paradise and this made me smile".[17]

Fatima died in the month of Ramadan, six months after the death of the Prophet. It is reported that Ali was not at home at the time of her death. Before her death, she asked for water and bathed and then she wore good clothes, then she asked for her bed to be made and went to bed facing Kabah. Umm Salamah was with her. She told her that the time of her departure had come and since she had already taken a bath, there was no need to give her a bath again after her death. Immediately after that, she died, [18] but it seems she was given a bath and as per her will she was buried the same night.

Fatima was very generous and considerate of the misery of others. A Jewish neighbor of hers embraced Islam but his relatives and friends did not like this act. In the meanwhile, his wife died. Nobody came forward to help him and to give a bath to his wife. When Fatima got this news, she immediately went to his house along with a slave woman and gave a bath to her. This shows her great concern for the neighbors and the needy.

Fatima had given birth to three sons and three daughters. Her third son Mohsin and her first daughter Ruqayya died in their childhood and that is why historians have not written much about them .Her second daughter Kulthum was married to Umar bin Khattab, when he was the Caliph and was in an advanced age. [19] The main reason for this marriage was that he wanted to be in the lineage of the Prophet. It may be observed that neither polygamy nor child marriage was a social stigma rather it was a part of Arab culture of that time.

Fatima was a perfect example of a very pious and devoted woman. The Prophet had pointed out that among men there have been many perfect, but among women, there were only four: Asia, the wife of Pharaoh, Mary the daughter of Imran, Khadijah the daughter of Khuwaylid and Fatima the daughter of Muhammad. Fatima had many titles such as Tahira, Mutahira, Zakia, Razia and Batul. All these titles reflect her multi-dimensional personality.

Grand Children Of The Prophet

S.No.	Name of the Mother	Name of the Child	Son / Daughter	Remarks
1.	Zaynab	Ali	Son	Died in childhood
		Ummamah	Daughter	Married to Ali after Fatima's death
2.	Ruqayya	Abdullah	Son	Died when he was about six years old.
3.	Fatima	I. Hasan	Son	
		II. Hussain	Son	
		III. Mohsin	Son	Died in infancy
		IV. Ruqayya	Daughter	Died in infancy
		V. Kulthum	Daughter	Married to Umar Khattab
		VI. Zaynab	Daughter	Married to Abdullah bin Jaffar

Prophet Muhammad(S) was greatly in love with children of not only of his kith and kin but also of others. Islam teaches that children are gifts of God and they should be taken care with love and affection, to ensure their healthy growth. In many of his teachings the Prophet emphasized the importance of showing kindness and compassion to children. Aisha has narrated that one-day a person from the desert came to the Prophet and said,"you are kissing children but traditionally we don't kiss them". The Prophet replied, "What can I do if God removed mercy from your heart?"

After Zayd's death, his youngest daughter, Zaynab on seeing the Prophet came running into his arms and started crying bitterly. The Prophet could not control his tears. When Sa'd ibn Usman asked him "O Messenger of Allah what is this?' The Prophet said, "This is one who loveth yearning for his beloved".

The Prophet placed special significance on playing with children. He encouraged parents to play with children. Not only did he use to play with his grandchildren but also with Aisha in the beginning of his marriage, in order to make her happy. He always enjoyed the company of Aisha's young friends who used to come to play with her.

From his daughters, he had nine grandchildren, five grandsons and four granddaughters, but three grandsons died in their childhood. The other five survived, got married and had their families

Zaynab, the eldest daughter of the Prophet had given birth to two children Ali and Ummamah. Ali died at a very young age, but the exact age is not known. There are different versions. Once or twice he was seen on the Prophet's camel. [20] There is another version that he had participated in the battle of Yarmuk in which he was martyred.

Ummamah was the eldest, granddaughter and since Ali, the grandson had died, she was the center of attraction for the Prophet. The Prophet loved her immensely. It is narrated that once someone presented a beautiful necklace to the Prophet, and the Prophet said he would give it to the one he loved most. Every one present was expecting that it would go to Aisha, as she was considered to be the favorite wife of the Prophet and the Prophet loved her very much, but the Prophet gave it to Ummamah. After the death of Fatima, Ummamah was married to Ali ibn Abu Talib [21]

The Prophet's second daughter Ruqayya had only one son by the name Abdullah but unfortunately he also did not survive for long. It is believed that he died at the age of six. The reason for his death was that a cock struck him with his beak into his eye. This caused a swelling of his face and poisoned his body, resulting in his death. [22] After this, Ruqayya did not have any other child. The Prophet's third daughter, Kulthum had no child.

The Prophet's youngest daughter, Fatima, had given birth to six children, three sons and three daughters. One son and one daughter died in their infancy. Fatima's eldest son, Hasan was born in Ramadan 3 AH[23] (625 AD). At the time of Prophet's death, he was about 7 years old. He had a very sharp memoray. He memorized the Quran and used to recite it daily. He remembered many sayings of the Prophet. He had 10 traditions to his credit.[24].When Fatima gave birth to second son in Shaban 4 AH[25] (626 AD) the Prophet was so pleased with the name of Hasan that he named the younger one as Hussain, which means the little Hasan (the little beauty). He was one year younger to Hasan. At the time of the Prophet's death he was about 6 year old . He also remembered 8 traditions of the Prophet. [26] It is narrated that when the third son was born to Fatima, Ali wanted to name him Harb, (battle) but the Prophet named him Mohsin. He died at a very young age.

The Prophet loved his grandsons greatly. History is full of incidents, which show his great love and affection for these children. Practically every day, the Prophet used to go to Fatima's house to see his daughter and grandchildren. Once when Hasan was just a kid, he came and embraced the Prophet, the Prophet prayed to God "O Allah, I love him; you may also love him and also love those who love him". Hasan and Hussain used to accompany the Prophet to the Mosque and many times while performing prayers they used to sit on his lap or back or on his shoulders.[27]He used to say that these are the flowers of my garden. Once the Prophet said that an Angel had given him the good news that Hasan would be the leader of the youth in paradise.

The Prophet gave time and attention to his grandchildren and tried to give them the right type of training as they were supposed to be the leaders of the young generation. Perhaps it was due to his training that they sacrificed their lives for the cause of Islam and made a name in history.

References and Notes

1. Abbasi, Madani, op. cit. p. 188.
2. Ashiqu Illahi, Maulana, op. cit. p. 18.
3. He was the son of Hala, who was Khadija's sister.
4. They were married, but had not come to live with their husbands.
5. Ashiqu Illahi, op. cit. p. 12.
6. Ibid.
7. Martin Lings, op. cit. pp. 158, 159.
8. Ibid, p. 235.
9. Usman bin Mazoom was a prominent companion of the Prophet and the first among the immigrants to die in Madina.
10. Martin Lings, op. cit. p. 163.
11. Ashiq Ilahi, op. cit. p. 27.
12. Yusuf Kandhlawi: Hayatus Sahabah Vol. I, op. cit., p. 322.
13. Ashiq Illahi, op. cit. p. 38.
14. Abbasi Madani, op. cit. p. 208.
15. Ibn Sa'd, Muhammad: The Women of Madinah, Ta-Ha Publishers, London 1997, p. 16.
16. Bukhari, quoted by Abbasi, Madani, op. cit., p. 214.
17. Ibid.
18. There is difference of opinion about her age at the time of death. Some believe that she was 29 years old, while some others state that her age was 24 or 25 years. The first seems to be more authentic: Shibli Nawmani, op. cit., Vol. I, p. 798.
19. Ashiqu Illahi, op. cit.p. 45.
20. Ibid. p. 17.
21. Ibid.
22. Ibid, p. 23.
23. Nawmani Shibli. Op. cit. vol. II p. 67.
24. Kandhlawi, Maulana Muhammed: Stories of the Sahabah, Idara Ishaat-e-Diniyat. New Delhi. p. 237
25. Naumani, Shibli, op.cit.Vol.II p.73
26. Kandhlawi op cit p 237
27. Ashiqu Illahi, op.cit p 45

Appendix I

Chronology of Events in the Life of Muhammad (P.B.U.H)

Brief Description of the Event	Approximate Date Age of the Holy Prophet according to Lunar Calendar	Approximate Gregorian and Hijra dates BH=Before Hijra, AH=After Hijra
The Holy Prophet of Islam, Muhammad, peace be upon him, born an orphan His father Abdullah, may Allah be pleased with him, had died a few months before the birth of his son.	0 years	9 or 12 Rabi-ul-Awwal 52 or 53 BH April 570 or 571 AD
Hadrat Halima Sadiyya, may Allah be pleased with her, appointed wet nurse.	8 days	
Return to Mecca under the care of his mother	6 Years	46 BH 577 AD
Mother, Hadrat Amina, may Allah be pleased with her, passes away	6 Years	46 BH 577 AD
Grandfather, Hadrat Abdul-Muttalib, may Allah be pleased with him, died	8 Years	44 BH 579 AD

First visit to Syria with a trading caravan 12 years 40 BH, 583 AD	12 Years	40 BH 583 AD
Pledge of Fudul to help the needy and the oppressed	15 Years	37 BH 586 AD
Second journey to Syria for trade as an agent of Hadrat Khadija, may Allah be pleased with her	25 Years	28 BH 595 AD
Marriage with Hadrat Khadija, may Allah be pleased with her	25 Years	28 BH 595 AD
Birth of a son, Hadrat Qasim (may Allah be pleased with him)	28 Years	25 BH 598 AD
Birth of his daughter, Hadrat Zainab, may Allah be pleased with her	30 Years	23 BH 600 AD
Birth of his daughter, Hadrat Ruqayya, may Allah be pleased with her	33 Years	20 BH 603 AD
Birth of his daughter, Hadrat Um-e-Kalthum, may Allah be pleased with her	34 years	19 BH 604 AD
Renovation of Ka'aba and the placement of Hajr-e-Aswad (Black Stone)	35 years	18 BH 605 AD
Birth of his daughter, Hadrat Fatima, may Allah be pleased with her	35 years	18 BH605 AD
Hadrat Jibrail bought the First Revelation in the Cave of Hira	40 Year	12 BH 610 AD
Revelation of the Holy Quran continues, Ministry of the Holy Prophet Muhammad (peace be upon him) is established. Hadrat Khadija (the wife), Hadrat Abu Bakr (the best friend), Hadrat Ali (the dearest cousin) and Hadrat Zaid (a freed slave and adopted son), may Allah be pleased with them all, accept Islam	40 Years 6 months	Friday 18 Ramadan 12 BH 14 August 610 AD

Open invitation to the people of Mecca to join Islam under Allah's command	43 Years	9 BH 614 AD
A group of Muslims emigrates to Abyssinia	46 Years	7 BH 615 AD
Blockade of Shi'b Abi-Talib	46 Years	7 BH 30 September 615 AD
Hadrat Hamza (paternal uncle) and Hadrat Umar, may Allah be pleased with them, accept Islam	46 Years	6 BH 616 AD
Hadrat Abu Talib, (beloved uncle and guardian) and only a few days later, Hadrat Khadija, the most beloved wife, may Allah be pleased with them, passed away	49 Years	Ramadan 3 BH January 619 AD
Marriage with Hadrat Sau'da, may Allah be pleased with her	49 Years	3 BH 619 AD
Marriage with Hadrat Aisha, may Allah be pleased with her	49 Years	3 BH 619 AD
Journey to Ta'if, about 40 miles from Mecca, for calling the citizens of Ta'if to Islam	49 Years	3 BH 619 AD
Journey of Mi'raj. Five daily prayers made obligatory for Muslims	50 Years	27 Rajab 2 BH 8 March 620 AD
Deputation from Medina accepts Islam	50 Years	2 BH 620 AD
First Pledge of 'Aq'ba'	52 Years	Dhul Haj, 1 BH 621 AD
Second Pledge of 'Aq'ba	52 Years	3 months BH June 622 AD
Hijra (migration) from Mecca to the cave of Thaur	52 Years	Friday 27 Safar 10 September 622

Emigration to Medina begins	52 Years	Monday 1 Rabi-ul-Awwal 13 September 622 AD
Arrival at Medina after the first Friday Prayer at Quba's Mosque	53 Years	12 Rabi-ul-Awwal 1st year AH 24 September 622 AD
Construction of the Holy Prophet's Mosque at Medina. Hadrat Bilal's call for Prayer (Adhan)	53 Years	1st year AH 622 AD
Brotherhood pacts between Ansar (Muslims from Medina) and Muhajirin (immigrants from Mecca)	53 Years	1st year AH 622 AD
Treaty with Jews of Medina	53 Years	1st year AH 622 AD
Permission to fight in self-defense is granted by Allah	53 Years	12 Safar 2 AH 14 August 623 AD
Ghazwa (Battle) of Waddan	53 Years	29 Safar 2 AH 31 August 623
Ghazwa (Battle) of Safwan	54 Years	2 AH 623 AD
Ghazwa (Battle) Dul-'Ashir	54 Years	2 AH 623 AD
Hadrat Salman Farsi, may Allah be pleased with him, accepts Islam	54 Years	2 AH 624 AD
Revelation and change of Qibla (direction to face for Formal Prayers, Salat) towards Ka'ba Fasting in the month of Ramadan becomes obligatory	54 Years	Sha'abn 2 AH February 624 AD
Ghazwa (Battle) of Badr	54 Years	12-17 Ramadan 2 AH March 8-13, 624 AD
Ghazwa (Battle) of Bani Salim	54 Years	25 Ramadan 2 AH 21 March 524 AD

Initiation of Eid-ul-Fitr and Zakat-ul-Fitr (Alms at the Eid-ul-Fitr).	54 Years	28 Ramadan / 1 Shawwal 2 AH 24/25 March 624 AD
Zakat becomes obligatory for Muslims	54 Years	Shawwal 2 AH April 624 AD
Nikah and Marriage ceremony of Hadrat Fatima, may Allah be pleased with her	54 Years	Shawwal 2 AH April 624 AD
Ghazwa (Battle) of Bani Qainuqa	54 Years	15 Shawwal 2 AH 10 April 624 AD
Ghazwa (Battle) of Sawiq	54 Years	5 Dhul-Haj 2 AH 29 May 624 AD
Ghazwa (Battle) of Ghatfan	54 Years	Muharram 3 AH July 624 AD
Ghazwa (Battle) of Bahran	55 Years	Rabi-us-Sani 3 AH October 624 AD
Marriage with Hadrat Hafsa, may Allah be pleased with her	55 Years	Shaban 3 AH January 625 AD
Ghazwa (Battle) of Uhad	55 Years	6 Shawwal 3 AH 22 March 625
Ghazwa (Battle) of Humra-ul-Asad	55 Years	8 Shawwal 3 AH 24 March 625 AD
Marriage with Hadrat Zainab Bint Khazima, may Allah be pleased with her	55 Years	Dhul-Haj 3 AH May 625 AD
Ghazwa (Battle) of Banu Nudair	56 Years	Rabi-ul-Awwal 4 AH August 625 AD
Prohibition of Drinking in Islam	56 Years	Rabi-ul-Awwal 4 AH August 625 AD

Ghazwa (Battle) of Dhatur-Riqa	56 Years	Jamadi-ul-Awwal 4 AH October 625 AD
Marriage with Hadrat Um-e-Salma, may Allah be pleased with her	56 Years	Shawwal 4 AH March 626 AD
Ghazwa (Battle) of Badru-Ukhra	56 Years	Dhul Qad 4 AH April 626
Ghazwa (Battle) of Dumatul-Jandal	57 Years	25 Rabi-ul-Awwal 5 AH
Ghazwa (Battle) of Banu Mustalaq Nikah with Hadrat Juwayriah bint Harith, may Allah be pleased with her	57 Years	3 Shaban 5 AH 28 December 626 AD
Marriage with Hadrat Zainab bint Hajash, may Allah be pleased with her	57 Years	Shawwal 5 AH February 627 AD
Revelation for Hijab, rules of modesty	57 Years	1 Dhi Qa'd 5 AH 24 March 627 AD
Ghazwa (Battle) of Ahzab or Khandaq (Ditch)	57 Years	8 Dhi Qa'd 5 AH 31 March 627 AD
Ghazwa (Battle) of Bani Quraiza	57 Years	Dhul-Haj 5 AH April 627 AD
Ghazwa (Battle) of Bani Lahyan	57 Years	1 Rabi-ul-Awwal 6 AH 21 July 627 AD
Ghazwa (Battle) of Dhi Qard or Ghaiba	58 Years	Rabi-ul-Akhar 6 AH August 627 AD
Treaty of Hudaibiyya	58 Years	1 Dhi Qa'd 6 AH 13 March 628 AD
Prohibition of Marriage with non-believers	58 Years	Dhi Qa'd 6 AH March 628 AD

Marriage with Hadrat Habiba, may Allah be pleased with her	58 Years	Dhul-Haj 6 AH April 628 AD
Invitation sent to various rulers to accept Islam	58 Years	1 Muharram 7AH May 628 AD
Ghazwa (Battle) of Khaibar Return of Muslims from Abyssinia. Marriage with Hadrat Safiyya, may Allah be pleased with her. Ghazwa (Battle) of Wadiyul-Qura and Taim.	58 Years	Muharram 7 AH June 628 AD
Performance of Umra (Umratul-Qada) Marriage with Hadrat Maimuna, may Allah be pleased with her	59 Years	Dhi Qa'd 7 AH March 629 AD
Hadrat Khalid bin Walid and Hadrat Umar bin Al-'Aas, may Allah be pleased with both, accept Islam	60 Years	Safar 8 AH June 629 AD
Ghazwa of Muta	60 Years	Jamadi ul Awwal 8 AH August 629 AD
Ghazwa (Battle) of Mecca and Fall of Mecca	60 Years	10 Ramadan 8 AH 1 January 630 AD
Ghazwa (Battle) of Hunain (or Autas or Hawazan) and Ghazwa (Battle) of Ta'if	60 Years	Shawwal 8 AH January 630 AD
Arrival in Ja'rana Deputation from Hawazan accepts Islam	60 Years	5 Dhi Qa'd 8 AH 24 February 630 AD
Regular establishment of Department of Zakat (Alms) and Sadaqa (Charity), and appointment of administrative officers	60 Years	Muharram, 9 AH April 630 AD
Deputation from Ghadra accepts Islam	60 Years	Safar 9 AH May 630 AD

Deputation from Balli accepts Islam	61 Years	Rabi-ul-Awwal, 9 AH June 630 AD
Ummul-Muminin Hadrat Mariya, may Allah be pleased with her, gave birth to a son, Hadrat Ibrahim, may Allah be pleased with him	61 Years	Jamadi-ul-Akhar, 9 AH August 630 AD
Ghazwa (Battle) of Tabuk, the last great battle lead by the Holy Prophet, peace be upon him	61 Years	Rajab, 9 AH October 630 AD
Ordinance of Jizya, tax on non-believers seeking protection from Muslims and exemption from military service in defense of the country they were living in as its citizens	61 Years	Rajab 9 AH October 630 AD
Pilgrimage journey of Hadrat Abu Bakr Siddique, may Allah be pleased with him	61 Years	Dhi Qa'd, 9 AH February 631 AD
Hajj (pilgrimage of Ka'ba in Mecca) made Obligatory by Allah Interest is prohibited in Islam	61 Years	
Deputation Tai, Hamadan, Bani Asad and Bani Abbas, all accept Islam	61 Years	
Deputation from Ghuttan accepts Islam	62 Years	Ramadan, 10 AH 631 AD
Departure from Medina for Mecca for Hajjatul-Wida (Farewell Pilgrimage)	62 Years	25 Dhi Qa'd 10 AH 23 February 632 AD
Entry into Mecca for Hajjatul-Wida (Farewell Pilgrimage)	62 Years	4 Dhul-Haj 10 AH 1 March 632 AD
Hajjatul-Wida, departure for 'Arafat, Farewell Sermon Received the last revelation from Allah	62 Years	Friday 9 Dhul Hajj 10 AH 6 March 632 AD

Return from Mana, Hajjatul-Wida	62 Years	13 Dhul-Hajj 10 AH 10 March 632 AD
Arrival of deputations from Nakha' Last deputation received by the Holy Prophet, peace be upon him	62 Years	15 Muharram 11 AH 11 April 632 AD
Sarya Usama bin Zaid, may Allah be pleased with him, last successful military mission during the Holy Prophet's life	62 Years	28 Safar 11 AH 24 May 632 AD
The Holy Prophet, peace be upon him, falls ill	62 Years	Monday 29 Safar 11 AH 25 May 632 AD
The Holy Prophet, peace be upon him, lead the last Salat four days before his departure from this world	62 Years	Wednesday 8 Rabi-ul-Awwal 11 AH 3 June 632 AD
The Holy Prophet, peace be upon him, offered his last Prayer in congregation in the Mosque lead by Hadrat Abu Bakr, may Allah be pleased with him	63 Years	Monday 12 Rabi-ul-Awwal 11 AH 7 June 632 AD
The Holy Prophet, peace be upon him, passed away	63 Years	Inna lillahe Wa Inna Elaihe Rajioon
Janaza (funeral) Prayer and burial	63 Years	Wednesday 14 Rabi-ul-Awwal 11 AH 9 June 632 AD

http://www.islam.com/chronolog.htm

Appendix II

The Prophet Muhammad's(S) Last Sermon

*This sermon was delivered on the **Ninth Day of Dhul Hijjah 10 A.H.** in the 'Uranah valley of Mount Arafat' (in Mecca).*

After praising, and thanking Allah he said:

"O People, lend me an attentive ear, for I know not whether after this year, I shall ever be amongst you again. Therefore listen to what I am saying to you very carefully and TAKE THESE WORDS TO THOSE WHO COULD NOT BE PRESENT HERE TODAY.

O People, just as you regard this month, this day, this city as Sacred, so regard the life and property of every Muslim as a sacred trust. Return the goods entrusted to you to their rightful owners. Hurt no one so that no one may hurt you. Remember that you will indeed meet your LORD, and that HE will indeed reckon your deeds. ALLAH has forbidden you to take usury (interest), therefore all interest obligation shall henceforth be waived. Your capital, however, is yours to keep. You will neither inflict nor suffer any inequity. Allah has Judged that there shall be no interest and that all the interest due to Abbas ibn 'Abd'al Muttalib (Prophet's uncle) shall henceforth be waived...

Beware of Satan, for the safety of your religion. He has lost all hope that he will ever be able to lead you astray in big things, so beware of following him in small things.

O People, it is true that you have certain rights with regard to your women, but they also have rights over you. Remember that you have taken them as your wives only under Allah's trust and with His permission. If they abide by your right then to them belongs the right to be fed and clothed in kindness. Do treat your women well and be kind to them for they are your partners and committed helpers. And it is your right that

167

they do not make friends with any one of whom you do not approve, as well as never to be unchaste.

O People, listen to me in earnest, worship ALLAH, say your five daily prayers (Salah), fast during the month of Ramadan, and give your wealth in Zakat. Perform Hajj if you can afford to.

All mankind is from Adam and Eve, an Arab has no superiority over a non-Arab nor a non-Arab has any superiority over an Arab; also a white has no superiority over black nor a black has any superiority over white except by piety and good action. Learn that every Muslim is a brother to every Muslim and that the Muslims constitute one brotherhood. Nothing shall be legitimate to a Muslim which belongs to a fellow Muslim unless it was given freely and willingly. Do not, therefore, do injustice to yourselves.

Remember, one day you will appear before ALLAH and answer your deeds. So beware, do not stray from the path of righteousness after I am gone.

O People, NO PROPHET OR APOSTLE WILL COME AFTER ME AND NO NEW FAITH WILL BE BORN. Reason well, therefore, O People, and understand words which I convey to you. I leave behind me two things, the QURAN and my example, the SUNNAH and if you follow these you will never go astray.

All those who listen to me shall pass on my words to others and those to others again; and may the last ones understand my words better than those who listen to me directly. Be my witness, O ALLAH, that I have conveyed your message to your people".

Glossory Of Islamic Terms

AH: After Hijra.It is the reference used in the Islamic calendar like A.D., which is used in the common calendar.

Adhan: The call for prayer. It is called five times a day.

Ahl-a–Suffah: The people of the platform. They were dedicated impoverished student of Islam who used to live in the Mosque.Their sole task was learning Qur'an and teachings of the Prophet.

Allah: The true name for the creator of the universe. Lord.

Ansar: Helpers. These were the people of Madina who responded to the Prophet Muhammad's(S) call to Islam and offered Islam a city-state.

Aqabah: A place just outside of Mecca in Mina, where the first Muslims from Yathrib (Madina) pleaged allegiance to the Prophet in the year 621.CE.

Asr: The late afternoon obligatory prayer.

Ayah: The Arabic meaning of Ayah is miracle and a sign. The Quran is considered to be a miracle itself. Each verse of the Quran is called Ayah

C.E.: It stands for Christian Era. It is used instead of A.D (*Anno Domini* or year of the Lord) in Islamic literature referring to the dates before the Hijra.

Dirham: A silver coin.

Fajr: The obligatory salah prayer before sunrise.

Fiqh: Knowledge and jurisprudence in Islam.

Iddat: Iddat has been defined as the waiting period for a widow or divorced. The waiting period means that after the cessation of nikah the woman has to restrain herself for another Nikah till the prescribed period is over.

Isha: Evening salah, which may be performed just over an hour after sunset until midnight.

Inna lillahi wa innailahi rajiun: We are from Allah and to home we are returning.When a Mslim is struck with calamity, or when he looses one of his loved one, he should say this statement.

Haj: It means the performance of pilgrimage to Mecca It is one of the five Pillars of Islam.

Halal: Something that is lawful and permitted in Islam.

Haraam: Something, which is unlawful or prohibited in Islam.

Itekaf: Seclusion to concentrate on prayer to Allah.

Jahiliyyah: Means ignorance. It refers to the pre-Islamic era existed in Arabia.

Kabah: The first house of worship built for mankind. It was originally built by Adam and later on reconstructed by Abraham and Ismail. It is a cubed shaped structure based in the city of Mecca to which all Muslims turn to in their five daily prayers.

Khutbah: A speech or sermon. It is usually referred to the sermon given during Friday prayer, Eid prayer, or marriage ceremony.

Momin: A person who has deep faith in Allah and is a righteous and obedient servant of Allah.

Munafiq: A hypocrite. One whose external appearance is Islam but whose inner reality conceals kufr.

Muharram: The first month in the Islamic calendar.

P.B.U.H.: These letters are abbreviations for the words Peace Be Upon Him.

Qiblah: It is the direction that Muslims face when they do their prayers. It is in the direction of the Kabah in Mecca

Quraish :The most powerful and prominent tribe in all of Arabia in the Prophet's era. The Prophet was from among the Quraish.

Rasul/Rasool: A messenger. Allah sent many prophets and messengers to mankind. 25 are mentioned in the Quran.

Rabi -al-Awal: The third month of Islamic calendar.

Rajab: The seventh month of Islamic calendar.

Sahabi: A companion of the Prophet. Plural, Sahabah.

Shaban: The eight month of the Islamic calendar.

Shariah: It signifies the entire Islamic way of life specially the law of Islam.

Shawwal: The tenth month of Islamic calendar.

Shirk: Associating partner with Allah.

Tahajjud: Voluntary prayer done in last part of the night.

Takbir: Saying Allahu Akbar. (Allah is the greatest)

Taraweeh: Prayers done after Isha during Ramadan, the fasting month.

Ummul Mumineen: Mothers of Faithful. A title given to each of the wives of the Prophet.

Umrah (minor pilgrimage): Is an Islamic rite and consist of pilgrimage to the Kabah.

Walima: A marriage banquet.

Zakah (Purifying Alms): Literary means purification. It refers to the mandatroy amount that a Muslim must pay out of his property. It is among the five pillars of Islam

Zam Zam: The sacred well inside Al Haram Ash-Shareef in Mecca.

The Other Books By The Author

In English
1. Management In A Princely State (Hyderabad)
2. Developments In Administration Under H.E.H. the Nizam vii
3. State Administration In Andhara Pradesh
4. Women In Indian Police
5. Women Police And Social Change
6. The Suicide---- Problems And Remedies
7. Women's Developments---- Problems And Prospects
8. Women, Peace and Security (In press)

In Urdu
9. Aks e kayanat
10. Sondhi Mitti Ka Ittar
11. Sitaron Say Aagay
12. Mera Paygham e Muhabat.
13. Shamim Aleem Say Milye (Edited)

About The Author

Born and raised in a distinctive Muslim family of India, her father was a member of the Indian Police. Shamim Aleem had the added advantage of spending bulk of her adult life in eciated cultural milieu of Hyderabad Deccan. It was the emphasis on girl's education, laid down by her parents that guided her and her offsprings life.

On her selection for a teaching assignment in the prestigious Osmania University (Hyderabad), she moved to Hyderabad, married another academic Prof. M.A. Aleem and continued her pursuit of knowledge and acquired a Ph.D in Personnel Management, besides her Masters Degrees in Political Science and Public Administration. She served Osmania University for 35 years, in different capacities such as Chairperson, Department of Public Administration, and Board of Studies and Member, University Academic Senate.

She has published twelve books and has contributed a large number of articles of academic values in national and international journals. She has conducted six research studies and organized a number of seminars. She was awarded a Fulbright Scholarship in recognition of her attainments, which enabled her to travel in the United States and meet academics of her discipline. Her area of specialization is Personnel Management with special reference to women.

After the demise of her husband, she migrated to the United States in 1996, where her children have settled.

She has since been writing short stories, human-interest features, columns and essays mainly in Urdu language. Leading Urdu papers and magazines have published almost all of them. Selected pieces have been brought out in four compilations that have received positive and laudatory reviews in the media.

For the last few years she has been working on the project Prophet Muhammad(S) And His Family, A Sociological Perspective, which has now taken the form of this book.